THE BOY
WHO
KICKED PIGS

Adapted by
Kill the Beast

Based on the novel by
Tom Baker

ISBN 978-0-573-13251-3
concordtheatricals.co.uk
concordtheatricals.com
Cover art © Oliver Baxter

FOR PRODUCTION ENQUIRIES

UNITED KINGDOM AND WORLD

EXCLUDING NORTH AMERICA

licensing@concordtheatricals.co.uk

020-7054-7200

NORTH AMERICA

info@concordtheatricals.com

1-866-979-0447

Each title is subject to availability from Concord Theatricals, depending upon country of performance.

This work is published by Samuel French, an imprint of Concord Theatricals. Ltd

The First-Class Rights in this play are controlled by Avalon Management Group Ltd, 4a Exmoor St, Ladbroke Grove, London W10 6BD.

No one shall make any changes in this title for the purpose of production. No part of this book may be reproduced, stored in a retrieval system, scanned, uploaded, or transmitted in any form, by any means, now known or yet to be invented, including mechanical, electronic, digital, photocopying, recording, videotaping, or otherwise, without the prior written permission of the publisher. No one shall share this title, or part of this title, to any social media or file hosting websites.

The moral right of Kill the Beast and Tom Baker to be identified as authors of this work has been asserted in accordance with Section 77 of the Copyright, Designs and Patents Act 1988.

USE OF COPYRIGHTED MUSIC

A licence issued by Concord Theatricals to perform this play does not include permission to use the incidental music specified in this publication. In the United Kingdom: Where the place of performance is already licensed by the PERFORMING RIGHT SOCIETY (PRS) a return of the music used must be made to them. If the place of performance is not so licensed then application should be made to PRS for Music (www.prsformusic.com.). A separate and additional licence from PHONOGRAPHIC PERFORMANCE LTD. (www. ppluk.com) may be needed whenever commercial recordings are used. Outside the United Kingdom: Please contact the appropriate music licensing authority in your territory for the rights to any incidental music.

USE OF COPYRIGHTED THIRD-PARTY MATERIALS

Licensees are solely responsible for obtaining formal written permission from copyright owners to use copyrighted third-party materials (e.g., artworks, logos) in the performance of this play and are strongly cautioned to do so. If no such permission is obtained by the licensee, then the licensee must use only original materials that the licensee owns and controls. Licensees are solely responsible and liable for clearances of all third-party copyrighted materials, and shall indemnify the copyright owners of the play(s) and their licensing agent, Concord Theatricals Ltd., against any costs, expenses, losses and liabilities arising from the use of such copyrighted third-party materials by licensees.

IMPORTANT BILLING AND CREDIT REQUIREMENTS

If you have obtained performance rights to this title, please refer to your licensing agreement for important billing and credit requirements.

THE BOY WHO KICKED PIGS was originally staged at The Lowry, Salford from the 21st-23rd June 2012, as part of The Lowry's In Development With scheme. Directed by Clem Garritty, Composer Ben Osborn, Video Design Bryan Woltjen, Costume Designer Nina Scott, Lightning Designer Elliott Griggs, Stage Manager Fergus Nimmo, Deputy Stage Manager Robyn Pawlow, Assistant Costume Design Rachel Schofield Owen, Assistant Composer Joe Campbell. The cast was as follows:

ROBERT CALIGARI, FRANK GRICE, JUNE, CASSIE, SUNBATHER 3, RADIO 4, BUS DRIVER, FATHER MATTHEW .... David Cumming

NERYS CALIGARI, BILLY, PHILIP BOTTERING, MRS MILK, NURSE, SUNBATHER 2, AGNES, EUNICE, ADMIRAL, RADIO 2, FATHER LUKE, MRS PARP .... Natasha Hodgson

TREVOR, OLD SEA CAPTAIN, THOMAS CROWE, PRIVATE, ROGER, DOCTOR, SUNBATHER 1, LONELY TOM, REGINALD, GERTRUDE, RADIO 3, FATHER JOHN, PARP JUNIOR, CALLUM THE RAT............................Oliver Jones

SALLY, WENDY HORSEBOX, CONSTABLE, TED, MRS CALIGARI, DAVE, PEDRO, JUANITA, BORIS, TERRY THE FERRET MAN, FILIDIA, RADIO 1, FATHER MARK, MR PARP, FELICITY THE RAT ....Zoe Roberts

CHARACTERS

Caligari household / Robert's lair
ROBERT CALIGARI – (M, 13)
NERYS CALIGARI – (F, 10)
TREVOR THE PIGGYBANK – (Voice Only)
MRS CALIGARI – (Voice Only)
CONSTABLE
PRIVATE

In the Wig and Thistle (all aged 70+)
FRANK GRICE
SALLY
BILLY
THE OLD SEA CAPTAIN

At the Kent Clarion
THOMAS CROWE
WENDY HORSEBOX
PHILIP BOTTERING – (M, 15)

Residents of Vampire Close
TED
JUNE
MRS MILK
ROGER

At the Doctor's office
DOCTOR
NURSE

At the beach
DAVE – (Voice Only)
CASSIE
PEDRO MAMIYA
SUNBATHER 1
SUNBATHER 2
SUNBATHER 3
JUANITA CHIHUAHUA

In the Wanted ads
AGNES
BORIS
LONELY TOM
EUNICE
TERRY THE FERRET MAN
REGINALD
FILIDIA
GERTRUDE
ADMIRAL

On the motorway
RADIO 1
RADIO 2
RADIO 3
RADIO 4
BUS DRIVER
FATHER MATTHEW
FATHER LUKE
FATHER MARK
FATHER JOHN
MR PARP
MRS PARP
PARP JUNIOR

In Robert's Lair
CALLUM THE RAT
FELICITY THE RAT

AUTHOR'S NOTES

It turns out we love horrible things. Writing *The Boy Who Kicked Pigs* was the ignition switch on what has become a ten-years-and-counting working relationship between the five of us, more often than not focussing on stories where something awful happens to a variety of weirdos.

Who knows whether it's the vandalism, murder, dismemberment, evisceration, impalement or incineration – something about Robert Caligari's blood-spattered final days resonated deep within us, drew us in to its pointy lair and quickly reminded us that people love chaos and carnage – especially when it's funny.

Adapting this bizarre story from Tom Baker's mind via the twisted pages of his novel taught us a lot about comedy, stagecraft and storytelling. For a first show, it presented plenty of challenges; staging the butchery of a shark, a colossal motorway pile up and a graphic, wet and splashy finale where a boy is eaten alive by debonair rats as an anniversary dinner. It also taught us to hang these moments on a story so that through the pink mist of mass slaughter, you can laugh but you can also, in some way, care about this strange boy in this odd part of Kent.

Ultimately, this story is about a lonely boy who's driven to terrible acts of violence by a talking piggy bank, mixing the truly dark and the utterly ridiculous. Everyone's horrible, and everyone gets their comeuppance. But we couldn't help but wonder whether, if Robert had someone else to talk to – a single real person to listen to him when he felt unheard and ignored – all the characters could have had much happier endings.

It would be less fun though.

CASTING NOTE

The play was written to be performed by a cast of four, which involved several quick changes (on stage and off) and each cast member playing several characters. We've noted how these roles can be divided up in our note on original casting. While it would be difficult to perform with a smaller cast, it could be scaled up very easily. Characters have been grouped by scene/location to make it easier to see where multi-roling is possible. Genders and ages have been added only for characters where it is important to specify. "Voice only" characters, including Trevor, were originally performed live into a microphone backstage.

The show is designed for multi-roling and for fast-paced, physical performances. As such, gender swapping is encouraged (and, if performed by a cast of four, necessary), not in order to create "drag" performances, but purely to encourage actors to create as broad a range of interesting and fun characters as possible, without being restricted to only playing characters of their own gender.

A NOTE ON RHYTHMIC SCENES

Community Service and Wanted are scenes in this play which are performed in a specific rhythm, sort of like spoken-songs. There is sheet music at the back of the script, giving the exact rhythms of the lyrics/lines. Please note: Where an x is used on the sheet music that denotes merely a rhythm and not the pitch of the vocals. Please feel free to be as outlandish and grotesque as you desire with the voice/tone/accent of your character, all that matters is the rhythm. It's as if the characters are merely talking as they usually do and it just so happens to be in toe-tapping time.

In terms of musical accompaniment, on each score we have provided a very basic skeleton of the musical bones of the scene. These are merely suggestions. If you wish to accompany the song with a full 80-piece orchestra please do so. If, like us when we created this show, you can only afford half a recorder and an old burnt shoe then by all means get a-tooting and a-booting! We encourage you to find your own way to "score" these not-quite-songs – it's just more fun that way. However, if you wish to follow in our original footsteps then we'd be equally as honoured.

Community Service: we have provided the bass-line used in the original production. This ran throughout the scene, stopping momentarily every so often to highlight moments of drama/comedy. Do with it what you will. And in terms of musical vibe, think *Cell Block Tango* from Chicago as performed by the residents of your Nan's weird care home.

Wanted: in the original production the chorus sang the word *"wanted"* as notated in the sheet music (C then A). Again, this is just a suggestion. Feel free to transpose this to a range that suits the performers, or choose a different melody altogether. We just ask that you keep this scene in a minor key. And when thinking of the vibe of this one, aim for a joyously evil fizz, like a gathering storm or the onset of a nasty migraine.

A NOTE ON DESIGN

The original stage production took place on a bare stage, in front of a series of projected backdrops, designed to look entirely like a living black-and-white comic book. The projections, props, set pieces, costumes and actors were all painted in shades of grey and the lighting used cold and blueish tones that heightened this greyscale effect. Gloomy levels and large shadows were employed to evoke early 20th-century horror cinema. Four mismatched stools of varying heights were used as furniture and to create certain locations.

ACKNOWLEDGEMENTS

A horrible little show about a horrible little murderer is an interesting gamble. Thank you to The Lowry, Salford – and specifically Porl Cooper and David Fry – for having faith in a pig-booting psychopath.

Not to bang on about The Lowry, but we would not have been able to make this, or indeed any subsequent show or other project together, were it not for their invaluable support. Thank you to Claire Symonds and Matt Eames for fighting not just for the survival, but for the immense success of emerging artists every day.

Thank you to David Byrne, Sophie Wallis, Helen Matravers and everyone at the New Diorama Theatre for saving us (and many like us) over and over again. What you do for theatre idiots with a dream and an extremely messy stage blood recipe goes above and beyond what anyone deserves. It's an honour to waste your valuable time.

Thank you to Tom Baker, for letting us push these delicious innards around.

Finally, to all those who lose themselves and find themselves in stories of carnage, chaos and coq au vin, thank you. The world is wilder, stranger and more magic for having you in it.

To weirdos everywhere.
And to all our parents, for letting us clog up the shed.

No Mum, you still can't throw anything out.

Scene One – Frank

(Darkness. A high-pitched female scream, all arch and old horror film.)

(Lights up as the scream continues and we see it is coming from the mouth of **FRANK GRICE**.*)*

(We are in the local pub, creaking and oaken. A stormy afternoon in Kent. **SALLY, BILLY** *and the* **OLD SEA CAPTAIN** *sit, enraptured by blind old* **FRANK GRICE**. *He needs to be visibly and obviously blind, a cane and sunglasses.)*

(He eventually wails to a close.)

FRANK. *(Finishing.)* – she said. The hot breath of the monster was bearing down upon her, fangs and claws gnashing against the young girl's pig-tailed visage. Grappling on the wet ground for a weapon, anything, my old hands closed around a great stone. I raised the rock above my head, and brought it down upon the beast, again, and again, and –

(He pauses to take a drink.)

– again! My face was wet with the blood and the rain, and silence fell. The beast was dead, and the girl was safe.

(They all applaud.)

BILLY. Incredible, bravo Frank!

FRANK. *(Approaching* SALLY.*)* No, no, you can't applaud murder, Billy, no matter how splended it is. I wiped my face clean of the monster's steaming innards, and swore that never again would I pit myself against the viciousness of the hungry badger. I took a life that day, and though, yes, I took it to save the life of little innocent Suzie Thompson, it will never sit easy in my old heart. So to remind myself of what I've done, of the price that poor creature paid, I kept the badger's pelt, that I cut from its lifeless corpse. Look.

> (**FRANK** *pulls out a long, braided pig-tail tied with a ribbon, obviously belonging to a little girl. The others gasp.*)

(Suddenly immensely cheerful.) So to answer your question, Billy, I haven't seen hide nor hair of the Thompson girl since. She didn't even say thank you, just scuttled off into the brush, growling and panting – probably still in shock, the poor thing.

SALLY. And her bod –

> (**BILLY** *nudges* **SALLY** *in the ribs.*)

Its body, Frank, what of that?

FRANK. Burnt it!

BILLY. Christ

FRANK. Burnt it, Sally! I stamped and stamped until its bones were crushed, and burnt it 'til it were dust. Cheers!

> (*He takes a drink from the vase on the table. The others go to stop him but he glugs it down.*)

Right, that's me, I best be off into the deadly traffic of the night.

BILLY. Good idea.

SALLY. Are you sure Frank?

FRANK. Yes, yes, now don't worry, I can see myself out, I know the way home like... *(Suddenly very sad.)* like the unending darkness of the void of blindness. *(Cheerful again.)* Oh well, always darkest before the dawn, as they say. Cheer-o. And hey, I've left a tenner behind the bar.

SALLY. Ten pounds? That's too much, Frank!

FRANK. Nonsense, nonsense, what's my motto? "If you're not dead –"

ALL. "– buy the drinks!"

FRANK. Exactly!

> *(The rest say their goodbyes, and* **FRANK** *exits, chuckling contentedly.)*

SALLY. I love that man. I always have. Remember how handsome he was? Before he lost his eyes in the Great Frost, searching for the children lost in the woods?

BILLY. We sing the song every year, Sally –

BILLY AND SALLY. *(Singing.)*
FRANK, FRANK, SUCH BEAUTIFUL EYES, BUT NOT ANY MORE 'COS THEY'RE GONE!

> *(They look into the distance, as if out of a window.)*

BILLY. There he goes now, look, waiting for a kind soul to tell him when to cross the road.

SALLY. Busy road tonight. Oh, here comes a lovely looking young lad to give him the all clear and lead him across.

BILLY. Probably a scout!

OLD SEA CAPTAIN. *(Ominously.)* Hmmm. Storm's brewin'.

SALLY. What's that?

ROBERT. *(Offstage.)* All clear Mr Grice!

> *(Screech of tyres as a vehicle brakes, a car horn, a smash and a thump.)*

> *(A stunned silence.)*

BILLY. ...Can we still use that tenner, or...?

> *(Blackout. Terrifying music*. Enter **ROBERT CALIGARI**. Centre stage, he catches **FRANK**'s cane, tossed from offstage. He laughs manically, then exits.)*

---

*A licence to produce THE BOY WHO KICKED PIGS does not include a performance licence for any third-party or copyrighted music. Licensees should create an original composition or use music in the public domain. For further information, please see Music Use Note on page 3.

Scene Two – Kent Clarion

(Either spoken or displayed visually: "One week earlier...")

(An old fashioned newspaper office. Old hands **THOMAS CROWE**, **WENDY HORSEBOX** *and young intern* **PHILIP BOTTERING** *are crammed together on a variety of seats of different heights.* **THOMAS** *is tapping away on a typewriter,* **WENDY** *is making notes. This is held for a few moments.)*

(The telephone rings.)

WENDY. *(Answering the phone.)* Hello, Kent Clarion newspaper, Executive Editor Wendy Horsebox speaking, anything dreadful happened? ...The classifieds, yes of course – *(To* **THOMAS.***)* incoming, Thomas!

THOMAS. Splendid, Wendy.

WENDY. Go ahead please sir, are you looking to buy, sell or exchange? *(Making notes.)* One skipping rope, mauve, in exchange for an earring...also mauve, lovely. An antique cheese grater for some...grass, yes. Seven satsumas in exchange for...four satsumas.

THOMAS. Did he just say – ?

*(***WENDY** *makes a shushing noise, though she's evidently excited. She pauses, listening.)*

WENDY. Thank you so much sir. Yes, yes of course, the ad will run in next week's edition. Alright, goodbye.

(She puts the phone down with reverence.)

THOMAS. Seven satsumas?

WENDY. For four satsumas!

THOMAS. He's done some bad maths there Wendy, and no mistake.

WENDY. I'm still shaking!

THOMAS. You'd never believe it, would you, if it hadn't just happened?

WENDY. I'd never believe it.

THOMAS. If it hadn't just happened I'd never believe it.

WENDY. What a world!

THOMAS. I tell you what, Wendy. That's a scoop.

(The truth dawns on **WENDY.***)*

WENDY. It is, isn't it!

THOMAS. You've scooped him there, Wendy.

WENDY. It's a proper scoop!

THOMAS. Oh yes, I'd say so.

WENDY. I'll get writing it up, Thomas!

THOMAS. There's not a moment to lose, Wendy, not for a scoop!

WENDY. This might be page four news!

THOMAS. Seven satsumas. In this day and age.

PHILIP. Excuse me?

THOMAS. *(Suddenly furious.)* What is it now?!

PHILIP. You still haven't given me anything to do.

WENDY. What are you here to do?

PHILIP. Work experience.

THOMAS. Well, do that.

WENDY. Yes. Do that.

PHILIP. But I can't just –

THOMAS. Thank you, dear.

WENDY. Thank you, dear.

(**PHILIP** *grabs a battered looking radio.*)

PHILIP. Well, do you mind if we put the radio on? It helps me think.

THOMAS. God have mercy.

WENDY. The radio...never in all my years... I–

THOMAS. There, there, Wendy.

PHILIP. So that's a "no", then, is it?

WENDY. Philip, this is the Kent Clarion. The Kent. Clarion. Not the Hertfordshire Herald and certainly not the Buckinghamshire Bugle.

(*They both spit forcefully onto the ground in disgust.*)

THOMAS. You'll not catch their presence in this office, no, sir. The heres and theres of the world with their *top stories* floating through the air like anthrax...with all their...scoops.

(*The telephone rings.*)

WENDY. (*Answering the phone.*) Hello, Kent Clarion newspaper, Executive Editor Wendy Horsebox speaking, anything dreadful happened? ...The classifieds? Yes of course – (*To* **THOMAS.**) Incoming, Thomas.

THOMAS. Splendid, Wendy.

WENDY. A correction? Oh yes, of course. (*Making notes.*) Seven satsumas, in exchange for...twelve satsumas.

(*The disappointment registers on both of their faces, there will be no scoop for* **WENDY.**)

No, no, that's fine. Thank you sir, I'll be sure to change the ad. Goodbye, goodbye.

(**WENDY** *hangs up, crushed.*)

THOMAS. Oh I am sorry, Wendy.

WENDY. No, Thomas, it's my own fault.

THOMAS. You were just excited about the scoop.

WENDY. That I was, Thomas, that I was. Lesson one, Philip: not every story will be a scoop!

PHILIP. Yes, yes, fine. I wonder if I could possibly be moved to the main news room?

WENDY. My dear boy, this is the main news room!

PHILIP. But...but all you do is classified ads.

THOMAS. *(Chuckling.)* So much to learn.

WENDY. Philip, have you ever *read* the news section of the Kent Clarion? Or the news of any local newspaper for that matter? There is no news. There is never any news. The most we can hope for is a natural disaster or a good set of classified ads.

PHILIP. That's ridiculous!

WENDY. Do you want to hear last week's stories?

THOMAS Don't make me read them, Wendy!

WENDY. There, there, Thomas. Last week's edition. Page four headline –

PHILIP. Why aren't your headlines on the front page?

WENDY. We don't bother with a front page, we find it raises expectations somewhat.

WENDY & THOMAS. "Start on page four"

THOMAS. That's *our* motto.

WENDY. So, pages four to five: local events. Pages five to seven: obituaries.

THOMAS. At least we've got death, Wendy.

WENDY. We'll always have death, Thomas. And then pages seven to twenty nine: the Classifieds!

THOMAS. Remember last week's top stories?

WENDY. Don't think about it Thomas.

THOMAS. "Local man has bath."

WENDY. I know, I –

THOMAS. "Pigeon trapped in shop again."

WENDY. Oh God!

THOMAS. There was one which just said: "Seasons: They're on the way!"

PHILIP. Surely something must happen around here.

WENDY. Nothing bad enough to warrant a front page, that's for sure.

PHILIP. But it doesn't have to be bad news!

WENDY. Oh my dear boy, lesson two:

WENDY & THOMAS. No news may be good news, but bad news is news!

PHILIP. What?

WENDY. People love disasters Philip. People love a good tale of maiming –

THOMAS. Of mauling –

WENDY. Of dark deeds and dastardly villains. Oh, what we'd give for a disaster!

PHILIP. That's a terrible thing to say!

THOMAS. One day, Wendy. One day!

(The telephone rings.)

(They all stare at the phone. Surely this is fate, surely this is the call!)

WENDY.   *(Full of anticipation.)* Hello, Kent Clarion. Anything...dreadful...happened? *(Beat.)* The classifieds? Of course. *(To* **THOMAS.***)* Incoming, Thomas.

THOMAS. Splendid, Wendy.

(A pause while **WENDY** *listens to the voice at the other end.)*

WENDY. I see, so that sounds like a simple exchange, a red hat for some pink plums?

Scene Three – The Caligaris'

(We are in the living room of the Caligari house. **ROBERT** *is reading the Kent Clarion Classifieds.)*

ROBERT. Stupid woman! I distinctly said a dead cat for some stink bombs! It's impossible working with amateurs.

*(**ROBERT** sits down, reading the newspaper.)*

Now, Mr Spotloop is still looking for a new watering can. So, there's no point stamping all over his precious flowers just yet then. No, let's wait 'til they grow a little. Fatty fat Mrs Birdie Truffle needs another bridle for her pony – that thing must be getting nearly as big as her!

*(**ROBERT**'s little sister **NERYS** enters, carrying **TREVOR**, an oversized, ugly piggy bank, and blowing a shrill screech on her recorder.)*

NERYS. What are you doing, Robert?

ROBERT. Nothing. Go away.

NERYS. Are you looking at your precious newspapers again?

ROBERT. No.

NERYS. Yes you are!

ROBERT. No, I'm looking at my precious newspapers and getting ready to stab you in the heart!

NERYS. Mum says you're not allowed to stab me in the heart!

ROBERT. Mum says that when you were born you were covered in thick black hair that the doctors had to shave every other hour and it only went away when they gave you an acid bath!

NERYS. When did she say that?

ROBERT. The other day. You were on the toilet.

NERYS. Liar!

(They growl at each other.)

(To her piggy bank.) Trevor, this is Robert. You must never, *ever* trust anything Robert says, because he's a nasty, filthy, rotten little liar who spends his entire summer holiday staring at classified adverts like a weirdo.

ROBERT. It's not weird.

NERYS. He spends all day cutting them out and cuddling them and taking them to his secret BLEEUGH –

ROBERT. Secret LAIR. And you're just jealous because you don't know where it is, and you'll never know. I'll die before I tell you, Nerys, and you know why? Because you WANT to know so much.

NERYS. Ignore him Trevor. He's just a sad, little weirdo who doesn't have any friends.

ROBERT. At least I don't pretend to have friends, like you with your stupid pigs.

NERYS. Don't listen to him, Trevor.

*(**ROBERT** addresses **TREVOR.**)*

ROBERT. Hello there. Are you my precious sister's new best friend?

NERYS. You're not allowed to touch him!

ROBERT. What, just like I wasn't allowed to touch Phyllis, the piggy lunchbox? Or Steven, your piggy hot water bottle? There was Kevin –

NERYS. Shut up!

ROBERT. Stanley –

NERYS. SHUT UP, ROBERT!

ROBERT. Penny, Felix, Jeremy the piggy-pot.

NERYS. Don't listen to him Trevor!

ROBERT. None of them lasted long though, did they, Nerys?

NERYS. Only because you RUINED them. You ruin everything I like and break it and destroy it because you're horrible.

ROBERT. A couple of good kicks from me and you're back to being lonely, lonely, sad, spindly, lonely, dribbly Nerys.

NERYS. *(Suddenly fearful, pleading.)* ...No.

ROBERT. YES.

    *(***ROBERT*** grabs* **TREVOR.***)*

NERYS. GIVE THAT BACK!

ROBERT. Why hello Trevor, aren't you a fine specimen!

NERYS. Robert, STOP IT!

ROBERT. I think Trevor wants to be *my* friend now Nerys!

NERYS. NO HE DOES NOT!

ROBERT. *(Pretending to listen to* **TREVOR.***)* What's that Trevor? Nerys smells like rotting leaves and fish pus and grease?

NERYS. He did NOT just say that!

ROBERT. That's not very nice, is it? Trevor needs to be taught a lesson.

NERYS. If you do anything to him, Robert, if you do anything I'll find your stupid lair and I'll... I'll...

ROBERT. You'll what? You'll find my secret lair when pigs fly.

NERYS. I'll find it!

ROBERT. Alright then, you asked for it!

>   (**ROBERT** *gives* **TREVOR** *a huge, swinging kick out of the window.*)

NERYS. NOOOOOOOOO!

>   (*Blackout.*)

Muuuuuuuuuuuuuum!

Scene Four – Coppers

(A door flies open and two police officers storm into view. **CONSTABLE** *is covered in fish. They deliver the following out to the audience, as if talking to* **ROBERT***'s mother.)*

CONSTABLE. Mrs Caligari! Apologies for bursting in on you like this, Mrs Caligari, particularly on such a lovely Sunday –

PRIVATE. Tuesday

CONSTABLE. After –

PRIVATE. Morning

CONSTABLE. After-morning, thank you Private.

PRIVATE. He's been hit on the head, Mrs Cali–

CONSTABLE. *(Accusatory.)* Mrs Caligari! My name is Detecting Chief Comfortable Inspective, and this is Private... Private... *(Struggles for the name.)* Well like I said, it's private, very hush hush!

PRIVATE. We're here to discuss the small matter –

CONSTABLE. Mrs Caligari, can you explain why a small piggy bank came sallying forth from your living room window earlier this morning?

PRIVATE. It appears that what's actually happened Mrs Caligari –

CONSTABLE. I was on my assigned rounds, Mrs Caligari, in my assigned squad car, minding the assigned business of mine and protecting that of others as is my earthly assignment, when a tin-plated missile of porcine extraction came flying in through the window and ploughed me in the...in the...

PRIVATE. In the face, sir.

CONSTABLE. In the face, Mrs Caligari!

PRIVATE. We have it on good authority that your son –

CONSTABLE. Luckily I managed to avoid a horrific accident, by steering my vehicle carefully and calmly into the back of a nearby fish van. Crisis averted.

PRIVATE. Mrs Caligari, if we could have a moment to–

CONSTABLE. Although...

PRIVATE. Sir –

CONSTABLE. Fish...everywhere!

PRIVATE. Sir, we decided –

CONSTABLE. Flukes, mackerel and halibut carpeted the road. Eels flew four sheets to the wind and then some.

PRIVATE. It's really besides the–

CONSTABLE. *(Remembering.)* God I can still see it. Gills flapping and flying like the heaving afterbirth of some mighty kraken. Nearby children covered in plaice. Nearby places covered in plaice. And as for the dog...

PRIVATE. ...the dog, sir?

CONSTABLE. The dog, private! A fiendish hellhound loosed amidst the chaos came flying at me, jaws agape, as only a pig terrier can!

PRIVATE. Pig?

CONSTABLE. What?

PRIVATE. Dog.

CONSTABLE. Dog, was it?

PRIVATE. Dog, sir, it was the pig that hit you.

CONSTABLE. A pig then, yes, it looked like a dog to me Private, but then in the heat of battle Mrs Caligari, even a mighty lion can look like a basket.

PRIVATE. George, why don't we go and have a lie down?

CONSTABLE. Determined to aid the fishmonger, weakened though I was by the blow to my...to my...

PRIVATE. Face?

CONSTABLE. Dog!

PRIVATE. What?

CONSTABLE. Indeed, I ran to the fellow's side, and skidded on a brazen bit of squid, Mrs Calamari –

PRIVATE. Cali*g*ari

CONSTABLE. *(To* **PRIVATE.***)* No thank you, I'm driving. *(To* **MRS CALIGARI.***)* – and I caught myself over what can only be described as a bone.

PRIVATE. Why don't we come back another time –

CONSTABLE. Before you could say "slicker than a mammoth's pelt at tea time", the dog had spotted the bone which was still in my grasp, and came full pelt towards me, determined to get its backbone –

PRIVATE. Bone back.

CONSTABLE. Scattering bananas –

PRIVATE. Fish!

CONSTABLE. *(To* **PRIVATE.***)* Probably! *(To* **MRS CALIGARI.***)* – as it went.

PRIVATE. And as for your son –

CONSTABLE. Yes, as for the *pig*, Mrs Caligari, I can promise you that the sum total of his innards – a tidy four pounds and seventy-six pence – will add very little to what is likely to be a hefty fining clean. Simon, I might add, is absolutely gutted...

PRIVATE. Simon?

CONSTABLE. Simon the fishmonger, private owner and chairman of Simon's Mobile Fish Palace. Gutted, he is. As gutted as his wares.

PRIVATE. Now, we don't want to imprison a lad as young as Robert –

CONSTABLE. The forms, Mrs Caligari, we'd be thigh-deep in papercuts before we'd even begun!

PRIVATE. But he will have to do some community service to make up the damages –

CONSTABLE. The fish!

PRIVATE. Some street sweeping ought to do it.

CONSTABLE. Everywhere!

PRIVATE. Picking up litter, that sort of thing

CONSTABLE. Like a massacre in an aquarium!

PRIVATE. He'll just have to do about twelve hours or so.

CONSTABLE. *(To* **PRIVATE.***)* Indeed he will, darling, indeed he will. *(To* **MRS CALIGARI.***)* And if you want your dog back, Mrs Caligari... *(Ominously.)* you've got quite a few bananas to find.

> *(***CONSTABLE** *exits.* **PRIVATE** *goes to add something further, but:)*

(Offstage.) Henry!

> *(***PRIVATE** *scuttles off.)*

> *(Blackout.)*

> *(A radio tuning in.)*

RADIO 1. *(Offstage, recorded if necessary.)* Welcome back to Petrol FM, Kent's prime-time traffic channel. Just a reminder to keep clear of Vampire Close today, as it's currently roped off for cleaning. Local fish-botherer Robert Caligari will be sweeping up salty sea guts all day today, so do pop by for a double whammy of gills and guilt. Onto our car mat question now, this week: Can you make soup out of them? Well, let's find out. Have you got that blender, Gordon?

> *(A blender whizzing up, blends into the opening notes of the next scene.)*

Scene Five – Community Service

*(A terrace of red-brick houses. Four weird and
wonderful nosy neighbours are lined up on
their front steps, peering out surreptitiously.
They are looking out towards the audience
where they can see **ROBERT** sweeping up the
mess made by the fish van incident as part
of his community service. The following
is somewhere between rhythmic dialogue,
poetry and glorious song.)*

[SONG: "COMMUNITY SERVICE"]

TED.

OI

JUNE.

PSST

MRS MILK.

THERE HE IS

ROGER.

LOOK

TED.

OI

MORNING THERE!

JUNE.

SHH

MRS MILK.

THERE HE IS

ROGER.

LOOK

JUNE.

ROBERT CALIGARI

TED.

OI

JUNE.

PSST

MRS MILK.

THERE HE IS

ROGER.

LOOK

TED.

THERE HE IS! OI!

MRS MILK.

MORNING WESLEY

JUNE.

SHH

MRS MILK.

THERE HE IS

ROGER.

LOOK

JUNE.

CLEANING UP HIS MESS

MRS MILK.

SWEEPING IT UP

TED.

CLEANING UP OUR STREETS

ROGER.

TRYING TO MEND HIS WAYS

ALL.

COMMUNITY SERVICE EY?

JUNE.

IT'S A LAUGH

MRS MILK.

SUCH A LAUGH

ROGER.

IT'S A HOOT!

ALL.

HA HA!

COMMUNITY SERVICE, EY?

TED.

I'LL TELL YOU WHAT IT IS JUNE

JUNE.

EY TED?

MRS MILK.

THERE HE IS

ROGER.

LOOK –

ALL.

HA, HA HA!

COMMUNITY SERVICE ...

TED.

...IS NO LAUGHING MATTER

JUNE.

OOH, SORRY TED

ROGER.

APOLOGIES FOR THE OUTBURST, TED

MRS MILK.

YOU DO VERY IMPORTANT WORK, TED.

(Various grumbles of agreement from others.)

TED.

OI

MRS MILK.

EH?

JUNE.

PSST

ROGER.

SHHH

ALL.

WHAT?

MRS MILK.

THERE HE IS

ROGER.

LOOK

JUNE.

LOOK

TED.

WHERE?

MRS MILK.

OVER THERE

ROGER.

OH THE ONE WITH THE HAIR?

JUNE.

NO BEHIND HIM, THE BOY WITH THE MOP AND THE EVIL
STARE

TED, MRS MILK & ROGER.

OHHHHHHHH

MRS MILK AND JUNE.

THERE HE IS

ROGER AND TED.

LOOK

MRS MILK.

CAREFUL THERE YOU'VE MISSED A BIT!

ROGER.

THE NASTY –

JUNE.

FILTHY –

MRS MILK.

ROTTEN –

(**TED** *lifts a finger to speak.*)

ROGER, JUNE & MRS MILK.

TED!

JUNE.

PUNISH HIM, MAKE HIM PAY,

MAKE HIM WORK FROM NIGHT 'TIL DAY;

MAKE HIM MOP, MAKE HIM SWEEP,

DON'T GIVE HIM ANY DINNER 'TIL HE CLEANS OUR
      STREETS;

FOR YEARS AND YEARS I'VE LIVED IN FEAR,

DUCKING OUT OF SIGHT WHEN ROBERT'S NEAR;

WHIP HIM, WORK HIM UNTIL HIS BACK BREAKS,

AND THEN WHEN HE'S DONE –

(*Sudden change from horribly sinister to
cheery neighbor.*)

– HE CAN HAVE A LOVELY BIT OF CAKE.

MRS MILK.

JUNE, JUNE, YOU ARE TOO GOOD TO THAT BOY, JUNE

ROGER.

THAT DOES SOUND NICE!

TED.

BATTENBERG?

JUNE.

NO, IT'S A BUNDT.

MRS MILK.

I ORDERED A BACON BUTTIE AND HE WAS IN THE QUEUE,
WHAT DID HE DO?

ALL.

HE KICKED IT

JUNE.

I WAS COOKING PORK CHOPS ON MY NEW BARBECUE,
AND WHAT DID HE DO?

ALL.

HE KICKED IT, KICKED IT!

ROGER.

I GAVE HIM A PIG-SHAPED TIN KAZOO, WHAT DID HE DO?

ALL.

HE KICKED IT, KICKED IT, KICKED IT!

TED.

I DRESSED MY BABY IN A PIGLET COSTUME, WHAT DID HE
DO?

REST.

HE – *(Gasp.)* – NO?!

> *(Whistling, they follow the path of the baby
> flying through the air.)*

TED.

WELL!

JUNE.

OH MY!

MRS MILK.

THERE HE IS

ROGER.

LOOK

TED.

WELL!

ROGER.
　　HUH!

MRS MILK.
　　IT'S WHAT HE DESERVES

JUNE.
　　OH MY!

MRS MILK.
　　THERE HE IS

ROGER.
　　LOOK

TED.
　　LOOK AT HIM THERE

JUNE.
　　WITH FISH IN HIS HAIR

ALL.
　　OH!

JUNE.
　　LOOK AT HIM SWEAR!

MRS MILK.
　　THERE HE IS

ROGER.
　　LOOK

TED.
　　JUST DESSERTS

MRS MILK.
　　INDEED!

ROGER.
　　HEAR HEAR!

TED.
　　SILLY BOY

JUNE.
OH, THERE HE'S SLIPPED. LOOK!

ALL.
HA!

JUNE.
LOOK AT HIM MOP

ROGER.
LOOK AT HIM HOSE

MRS MILK.
WITH COD IN HIS SHOES

TED.
AND SQUID UP HIS NOSE

JUNE.
HOW SILLY IT LOOKS

ALL.
IT SERVES HIM RIGHT

MRS MILK.
CLEANING UP AFTER

ROGER.
HIS PIGGY BANK'S FLIGHT

ALL.
HA!

(The following four lines are repeated in canon simultaneously.)

TED. *(Repeated.)*
TUT TUT

JUNE. *(Repeated.)*
SHHH

ROGER. *(Repeated.)*
SHAME

MRS MILK. *(Repeated.)*
THERE HE IS

ALL.
LOOK

TED.
TUT TUT

JUNE.
SHHH

ROGER.
SHAME

MRS MILK.
HA HA!

ALL.
THERE HE IS!
LOOK!

(They all fall about laughing.)

Scene Six– Doctor's

(The menacing beep of a far off heart monitor.)

(The **DOCTOR** *enters, confident, looking fantastic, and puts on his medical coat.)*

DOCTOR. Next!

(The **NURSE** *– a melodramatic, besotted damsel – leads in* **ROBERT.***)*

NURSE. Robert Caligari, Doctor, the boy who kicks pigs!

DOCTOR. The boy who licks prigs, you say?

NURSE. Kicks pigs!

DOCTOR. Licks prigs...well, it's that time of year again.

NURSE. Kicking, Doctor.

DOCTOR. But why would you want to kick a prig?

ROBERT. Pigs! I kick pigs.

DOCTOR. And who the hell are you?

ROBERT. Punter of porkers. Booter of bacon sandwiches. Champion striker for West Ham! ...Examine me sir, if you dare!

DOCTOR. Oh I intend to my boy! I intend to examine you very deeply. Chart, Stephanie?

NURSE. *(Reading from a clipboard.)* Caligari, Robert – thirteen years old, average height and weight though unusually angular for a boy his age. Several disturbing instances to date. He kicked a packet of quality sausages at the butchers' counter, booted the prize hog at the local County Fair, toe-punted his sister's piggy bank into a local policeman's face!

DOCTOR. It is clear the boy's obsessed! Let's begin the eggs-ham-and-bacon–

ROBERT. What?

DOCTOR. The examination. Lift your shirt please, my boy.

> *(He does. They recoil in horror.)*

That's enough Robert – there are ladies present. Okay – *(Using stethoscope.)* this just goes here then, on your *(Puts it on his cheek.)* flesh.

ROBERT. What?

DOCTOR. Well, your red pipe water –

ROBERT. You mean my blood?

> *(**NURSE** screams in disgust.)*

DOCTOR. Don't be obscene, boy!

ROBERT. Are you sure you're a doctor?

> *(**DOCTOR** and **NURSE** laugh.)*

DOCTOR. Oh yes, yes. I doct. Studied <u>docting</u> for years, marvelous pasttime, lots of graphs. You're in safe hands with me, my boy. Face!

> *(**NURSE** tips **ROBERT**'s face into **DOCTOR**'s outstretched open hand. He holds it, considers the weight of **ROBERT**'s head.)*

...Hmmm, Saggittarius.

ROBERT. What? No, I'm a –

> *(**DOCTOR** holds up a stethoscope to **ROBERT**'s mouth.)*

DOCTOR. Say "Ah".

ROBERT. Ahhhhhhh.

(**DOCTOR** *leaps back from the deafening noise of the amplified sound from* **ROBERT**.)

DOCTOR. Holy Jehovah!

NURSE. Diagnosis, Doctor?!

DOCTOR. No, no, no, it's definitely not diagnosis, I know that much. In fact, there's nothing physically wrong with the boy. His mucus is strong and aptly pungent and he's as nimble as a jaybird in spring! No no, the problem appears to be purely psychosomatic!

ROBERT. What?

NURSE. Who?

DOCTOR. Psychosomatic, an intellectual inability to implicate identity into indecision. It's all in Holbenstein! *(Accusingly.)* Did you read Holbenstein?

NURSE. I like the romance books!

DOCTOR. Nevertheless! Nevertheless. There is an issue here, it's plain to see. Young Robert simply has a passion, an unbridled need to...for want of a better word...

ROBERT. Boot Boars?

NURSE. Sock sows?

DOCTOR. To kick pigs, Stephanie! To kick pigs! It's a need! An animal instinct!

NURSE. But why? Why?

ROBERT. It's my sister, Nerys –

DOCTOR. That is a question that I cannot answer. I may be all-powerful, Stephanie, but I am still a mere mortal, no, no. The solution to this particular riddle lies in the cavernous mind of young Robert here. Why does he enjoy...kicking pigs?

ROBERT. Like I said, because...

DOCTOR. I mean, the boy doesn't know! And how could he? He's just a child!

NURSE. A child that's becoming a monster!

DOCTOR. Now now, yes yes, no no. I'm going to give you my professional medical opinion. Which is, we must listen to Robert...

ROBERT. Prepare for your minds to be well and truly boggled then. It all began when –

DOCTOR. – We must listen to him! Listen to his urges, let the disease guide our treatment.

NURSE. Then there's nothing we can do...

DOCTOR. There rarely is, my sweet, sweet, Stephanie, that's the harsh truth of docting.

(**ROBERT** *screams with frustrated anger.*)

But we mustn't blame ourselves, why if I had a thrup'ney bit for every young boy who came to me with destructive tendencies, I'd have half a crown-shilling and two bob tuppence and speak no more about it!

(*The* **DOCTOR** *spins the* **NURSE** *in a passionate dance, then throws her away like a piece of rotten meat. She lands. A moment of stillness.*)

Now, take this psycho back to the ward. Go and get yourself cleaned up and come back to me as pretty as a pony. And Robert, for God's sake boy –

(*He holds out a huge lollipop.*)

– take a lollipop.

(**ROBERT** *takes it, licks it and storms out.*)

A boy who kicks pigs, eh, whatever next. What is my next appointment, nurse?

NURSE. Well the girl who nicks figs has had to cancel, something about an arrest in a grocery shop in Margate, but your three o'clock, Mrs Bracken is already waiting outside.

DOCTOR. And what's wrong with her?

NURSE. She sicks up twigs.

Scene Seven – The Lair

(**ROBERT** *is sitting in his lair, which lies deep in the bottom of a burnt-out tree stump, filled with nasty looking spikes. He is hunched on a stool, all angry elbows and knees. He is reading the Classifieds in the newspaper, for comfort, and the top half of his body is at first obscured behind the over-sized Kent Clarion he has open. He tries to calm himself with Classified ads, it's a kind of therapy, but is constantly pulled back to his rage at being laughed at by the locals.*)

ROBERT. Those stupid, mindless, bloated, jelly-brained imbeciles! ...How dare they, how dare they laugh at me? One day I'll show them, I'll make them – Ooh! Wanted: Gertrude Winkleflap seeks brand new plate in exchange for some broken ones. Knew that would never work out. So the broken plates stay in play. (*Gasps.*) Wanted: Eunice Staunton seeks roller skates in exchange for –

(*Enter* **NERYS** *with a horribly shrill blast on recorder. She is holding the end of a thread.* **ROBERT** *jumps, but keeps the paper open in front of him.*)

Nerys! What are you doing in my secret lair? How did you find me?

NERYS. It was easy.

(*She holds up the end of the thread she followed.* **ROBERT** *lifts the newspaper to reveal that his jumper has unraveled and now comes only halfway down his chest. He lowers the paper.*)

ROBERT. Curses. Note to self: Nerys has grown a brain.

NERYS. I told you we'd find it Robert. Trevor and I are far too clever for you to hide from us.

ROBERT. Oh Trevor's here too? Good, I've really missed him.

NERYS. What is this place Robert?

ROBERT. It is my secret lair.

NERYS. It's just the inside of a tree stump. It's all dirty and dark and smelly, and Trevor nearly hurt himself on the spikes on the way down.

ROBERT. Shut up! Shut up and remove yourself from the lair, I'm busy with important busyness.

NERYS. Robert, what are you doing?

    (**ROBERT** *ignores her. A beat.*)

Robert, can I do it? Robert, I want to do it.

    (*He continues to ignore her. She is unbelievably irritating.*)

Robert I've got a new tune! Do you want to hear my new tune? Robert I'm bored. Robert I'm hungry. Trevor's hungry. Robert, I need a weeeeeeeee!!!

ROBERT. Shut up! Take this, but just shut up!

    (*He hands her a section of the paper.* **NERYS** *starts to read.*)

NERYS. "Obituaries" ...oooh look Trevor, some lovely stories for us to read! "Simon the fishmonger, of Simon's Mobile Fish Palace, was found dead in his own home. Simon's fish van business closed down last week after it was unable to recover from a disastrous incident involving a dog, a police car and...a piggy bank. *(Gasp.)* Trevor! Police confirm that Simon sat down to a four course fish dinner on Monday evening, before pegging a weight to his nose, and diving headfirst into his own lobster tank".

ROBERT. Wow.

NERYS. Robert...

ROBERT. Trevor's a murderer!

NERYS. No he's not! *(She suddenly realises.)* <u>You</u> are Robert! You're the one who kicked Trevor in the first place. If it wasn't for you, none of this would have happened.

> *(Beat as this sinks in.)*

ROBERT. You're right... I killed him.

> *(He stares for a moment before breaking out into a huge grin, laughing maniacally.)*

Hahaha! I killed him,I killed him! It was me!

NERYS. I hate you Robert Caligari! You're a murderer and I'm – I'm...telling Mum!

> **(ROBERT** *just laughs with triumph.* **NERYS** *runs off, sobbing into her recorder, leaving* **TREVOR** *behind.)*

ROBERT. I did it. I did it!! Oh the glory! Robert Caligari, giant amongst midgets. Robert Caligari, smiter of the ignorant and the silly. Robert Caligari... Murderer!

TREVOR. You're not a murderer.

> **(ROBERT** *reacts to the phantom voice, but does not realise it is* **TREVOR** *speaking. He looks around for the source of the voice.)*

ROBERT. Oh yes I am!

TREVOR. Don't be silly. You just kicked a pig, you didn't do any real murdering there.

ROBERT. He's dead, and it's my fault, so I did it!

TREVOR. Didn't. You've never done anything except dance to the tune of everyone around you, whimpering and sneering but never acting.

> (**ROBERT** *walks passed* **TREVOR** *to pick up the newspapers.*)

Don't walk away from me when I'm talking to you!

> (**ROBERT** *freezes.*)

ROBERT. What?

TREVOR. It's polite to face your opponent in conversation, Robert.

> (**ROBERT** *turns slowly to face* **TREVOR**.)

ROBERT. Are you...?

TREVOR. Yes Robert, it's me. Trevor.

ROBERT. Nerys...?! This isn't funny!

TREVOR. It's not Nerys doing this.

ROBERT. That's just what Nerys would say.

TREVOR. No, Nerys would whimper and play that God-awful recorder of hers.

ROBERT. You don't like her recorder?

TREVOR. Who does?

ROBERT. Not me.

TREVOR. Me neither.

ROBERT. I can't believe you think that, too!

TREVOR. I think what you think.

ROBERT. No-one thinks what I think.

TREVOR. You can't know that.

ROBERT. The day I take life lessons off a piggy bank...

TREVOR. You should always listen to your elders, Robert.

ROBERT. You're not my elder, you idiot. You're Nerys' piggy bank!

TREVOR. And before that I belonged to the Bishop of Crawley! And before that I was a paperweight for the Headmaster at Stowe. And before that... I was a bicycle. So you see, I've seen things my boy. I've heard things. You should show more respect.

ROBERT. Don't patronise me, pig. You're just a pig, pig. A tin pig.

TREVOR. Full of gold! And you, Robert Caligari, are full of cowardice!

ROBERT. Am not!

TREVOR. Prove it!

ROBERT. How? I know, I'll kick you! I'll kick you into another police van!

TREVOR. Ah, but that's not bravery, that's just sport. A real murderer doesn't leave anything to chance. A real murderer looks deep into the eyes of his victim, and makes a pact with the soul he is about to claim!

ROBERT. So you're saying...

TREVOR. I'm saying that, like so many things in life – omelettes...sleeping...digging holes – you can't do murder by halves! You have to give it some welly, look directly down the barrel of the gun. Select your victim, and act.

ROBERT. Well, if Simon the fishmonger doesn't count, then who?

(**NERYS** *re-enters.*)

NERYS. Robert, have you seen Trevor anywhere? Oh, there he is. We'll go now, and leave you with all of your no friends.

*(**NERYS** exits, **TREVOR** under her arm.)*

TREVOR. Remember, Robert...

*(An evil grin spreads across **ROBERT**'s face.)*

ROBERT. *(Gleefully.)* Let's put a cork in that recorder once and for all!

Scene Eight – Pedro

*(**PHILIP** sits in the Kent Clarion office, reading newspapers, searching for some exciting news.)*

PHILIP. Local man cures hunger! ... *(He turns the page.)* ...by eating a bun. Well, that's just...nice. That's news. Good news. Good.

(He looks around, he is alone. This is his chance to practise. He makes a noise imitating a phone ringing.)

Brrrp brrrp! Brrp brrrp! Hello! Kent Clarion! Philip Bottering speaking, what's your news please?

(He sighs. He can do better.)

No, it's not quite... Brrp brrp! Brrp Brrp! Hello Kent Clarion, this is Bottering, GO!

(Still not right. He is forlorn. Sadly, he tries once more.)

Brrrp brrrp. Brrrp Brrrp. Hello Kent Clarion, anything dreadful happen? Of course not, because nothing happens in Kent! Oh the classifieds, of course, incoming Thomas! Splendid Wendy!

*(He slams down his imaginary phone, frustrated and furious. Beat. Guiltily, he looks at the radio, checks nobody is watching and turns it on. A voice, **DAVE** the DJ, breaks through the static.)*

DAVE. *(Offstage.)* ...and that was *Killing Me Softly* which concludes our euthanasia special. Now, from one murder to another – I'm sure we're all sick and tired of hearing the headline "SHARK EATS SWIMMER",

I know I am! But how about "SWIMMERS MAUL SHARK"? Now there's a story with some real bite!

PHILIP. Swimmers maul shark!? That's terrible, how utterly–

DAVE. *(Offstage.)* We join Cassie live at the scene. Cassie.

(**CASSIE** *enters.*)

CASSIE. Dave.

DAVE. *(Offstage.)* Cassie.

CASSIE. Dave.

DAVE. *(Offstage.)* Cassie.

CASSIE. Thanks Dave. You join me live at "South Africa Beach" at Butlin's Holiday Park in Bognor. Normally a place for good old fashioned British seaside merriment such as donkey slapping, dwarf tossing and contracting tetanus, this beautifully mediocre setting has in the past week been the scene of a harrowing turn of events, following the disappearance of South Africa Beach's number one lifeguard, the shockingly handsome Pedro Mamiya. Mamiya. Mamiya. Mamiya. Mamiya...

> (**CASSIE***'s voice becomes warped, as though in an old film, and* **PHILIP** *is slipping into some sort of dream state. The Kent Clarion office becomes Butlin's "South Africa Beach".*)

> (*Music, a sixties guitar riff plays**. *We're on a beach.* **PEDRO***, horribly buff and horribly dumb enters like he's headlining at Glastonbury.*)

---

* A licence to produce THE BOY WHO KICKED PIGS does not include a performance licence for any third-party or copyrighted music. Licensees should create an original composition or use music in the public domain. For further information, please see Music Use Note on page 3.

PEDRO. Hey ladies, what's up? It's me, Pedro! Yo! Hey! Hey, you! Hey! Hey! You! Yooooo! How you doing? ... It's time for Pedro's Rules of the Beach! Rule number one: no swimming! It's like my father always used to say, treat the waves like you would a teenager: you can look...but do not touch! (*He laughs heartily to himself.*) Rule number two: no shouting, no shanking, no shipping containers of any kind (*Points at somebody offstage.*) yes I'm talking to you, Karen. Cazzo! Rule number three: keep your kids on a leash and your fat women in the shadows – people are trying to eat! Finally, remember, here at South Africa Beach, every day is Ladies Night. Free shots of salty sea water all round. Come on down! OK I go get a delicious chicken wrap now, be right back just don't drown ok?

> (**PEDRO** *exits.*)

> (**TWO SUNBATHERS** *enter half hidden behind a towel. As they talk they take it in turns to get changed behind the towel.*)

SUNBATHER 1. Ey love, isn't that Pedro a cracker eh?

SUNBATHER 2. I know! I thought my Brian was a hot potato but he's got nothing on Pedro. He's been gone so long.

SUNBATHER 1. I know, it's like winter in my heart when he's not around. Where is he by the way?

SUNBATHER 2. Has anyone seen Pedro? Anyone? Oh my God, Pedro is missing!

> (**SUNBATHER 3** *pops up from behind the towel.*)

SUNBATHER 3. Here, look what I've just found washed up on shore! A delicious chicken wrap... with extra cheese!

> (**SUNBATHER 3** *disappears back behind the towel.*)

SUNBATHER 2. The Pedro Special

SUNBATHER 1. El especial del Pedro

SUNBATHER 2. Then that means...

SUNBATHER 1. Look, I saw a fin out to sea, there's a shark!

SUNBATHER 2. A great white shark, just off shore!

> *(Pause.* **SUNBATHER 1 AND 2** *do a double take.)*

SUNBATHER 1 AND 2. *(Hysterical.)* Oh. My. God. PEDRO'S BEEN EATEN BY A SHARK!

> *(***SUNBATHER 1 AND SUNBATHER 2** *run off, terrified.)*

CASSIE. Delirious with sunburn, the busy bustling beach began to run a murmur and amok with news of the untimely death of Pedro Mamiya. Then all of a sudden a cry was heard along the sound.

> *(The* **BATHERS** *are back, tooled up with sharpened sand shovels and trowels.)*

SUNBATHER 2. Oh my God, that's the one! That's the shark that killed Pedro!

SUNBATHER 3. It's beached, it's beached!

SUNBATHER 1. How can you tell?

SUNBATHER 3. It's on the beach!

SUNBATHER 1. No, how can you tell it's the one that killed Pedro?

SUNBATHER 2. It's eyes! Look in its death-filled eyes!

SUNBATHER 1. MURDEROUS EYES!

> *(All recoil from the shark's glare.* **PEDRO** *crosses behind them, totally unnoticed, singing and dancing to himself.)*

(**PEDRO** *singing badly*.*)

SUNBATHER 3. Maybe he's still in there, all wrapped up like a Pedro tortilla

ALL. El speciale del Pedro?

SUNBATHER 2. Save Pedro!

SUNBATHER 3. Kill the shark!

SUNBATHER 1. Kill it 'til it's dead!!!

(*Pause.*)

ALL. Kill it!

(*The **BATHERS** charge forward and begin to hack the shark to death in slow motion.*)

CASSIE. They ripped and they tore, they screamed and they swore. The frenzy mounted, and the shark became a bloody pulp. One man even did a small wee in the shark's now empty eye-socket. Truly appalling scenes.

(*The mob exit.*)

We caught up with one of the mob, Juanita Chihuahua. Juanita, just juan question – why?

JUANITA. I loved Pedro. Very deeply. He took me to watch the stars one time in his car with his busy hands and my virgin heart and it was the most beautiful experience of my life. Today I removed the shark's stomach, for my beloved Pedro. He was not in there. He was not in there at all! All I found was a watch and some partially digested hula hoops. Long live the ghost of Pedro Mamiya.

---

* A licence to produce THE BOY WHO KICKED PIGS does not include a performance licence for any third-party or copyrighted music. Licensees should create an original composition or use music in the public domain. For further information, please see Music Use Note on page 3.

(JUANITA exits.)

CASSIE. And all of this because of a man people loved to love, and that man, Dave, was Pedro Mamiya, Mamiya, Mamiya, Mamiya...

> *(We are back in the office, and PHILIP cannot believe what he just heard.)*

PHILIP. That was... AMAZING!! I mean...awful, terrible, that poor shark, but –

> *(Pause. PHILIP can resist no longer.)*

Oh, who cares?! It was BRILLIANT news!

> *(THOMAS shouts from offstage, PHILIP quickly hides the radio as he speaks.)*

THOMAS. *(Offstage.)* Young man! They were out of cheese and pickle so I got you spam and spam instead. Hope that's okay!

PHILIP. Oh, yes, fine, thank you.

> *(PHILIP dejectedly sits down.)*

Please let something happen. Please.

Scene Nine – Weedkiller

(NERYS' room. The door creaks open, and **ROBERT** *can be heard, before he creeps in.* **TREVOR** *is balanced carefully on a chair in a splendid bonnet, in the midst of an abandoned tea party.)*

ROBERT. *(Initially offstage.)* Nerys? Oh Nerys? It's your favourite brother, Robert. Nerys, come downstairs, I've made you a delicious *(He enters and looks around.)* ...Where is she!?

TREVOR. Gone!

*(**ROBERT** rushes to **TREVOR**'s side.)*

ROBERT. Gone? Where? Is she sick? Is she dying? Was she rushed to hospital screaming and crying and – ?

TREVOR. No.

ROBERT. Then where?

TREVOR. Far worse than that. Recorder lesson.

ROBERT. ARGH! Why isn't it working?

TREVOR. You have to be patient, Robert.

ROBERT. I've been patient. It's been days now, days and – Are you wearing a bonnet?

TREVOR. Well, it's a tea party Robert, the invitation said smart casual.

ROBERT. You're supposed to be on my side!

TREVOR. Yes, but I'm a terrible patsy for a cream horn.

ROBERT. Trevor!

TREVOR. Ohh, very well, disrobe me then, boy and let us get down to brass tacks.

*(**ROBERT** removes **TREVOR**'s offensive bonnet during the following.)*

ROBERT. So, I've given her three doses, three – according to the manual she should be trying to scoop her own guts back into her body by now

TREVOR. You did get arsenic, didn't you?

ROBERT. What?

TREVOR. You got the premium, top-dog arsenic, like I told you

ROBERT. Well...

TREVOR. Oh Robbie

ROBERT. I bought weedkiller! Because Nerys is a weed.

TREVOR. And you're rubbing it directly into the corneas, I presume?

ROBERT. Well, no, I –

TREVOR. Or placing under the tongue, perhaps?

ROBERT. No. I'm more putting it directly into her –

TREVOR. Yes?

ROBERT. – cornflakes. At breakfast. Poison breakfast!

TREVOR. I'm beginning to wonder about you, Robbie.

ROBERT. What?

TREVOR. I'm beginning to wonder whether there's enough hate behind those cheeks of yours to carry out this task. Maybe you like this Nerys. Is that why you can't kill her?

> *(**ROBERT** grabs **NERYS**' recorder and points it at him threateningly.)*

ROBERT. Take that back!

TREVOR. Maybe little Robbie loves his sistery wistery

ROBERT. How dare you say that to me! How dare you – *(Looks at recorder in his hand.)* hang on, didn't you say she was at recorder lesson?

NERYS. *(Offstage.)* Mum, I'm just going to get my recorder!

> **(ROBERT** *hurriedly places the recorder back where he found it, and rushes to the door. It's too late.* **NERYS** *enters.)*

Robert?! What are you doing in my *(She gasps, and covers her eyes.)* why is Trevor naked?

ROBERT. He...he didn't want to wear it

NERYS. Robert!

ROBERT. He hates it!

TREVOR. Steady on Robbie, it does bring out my eyes

NERYS. *(Unaware of* **TREVOR**'s *voice.)* You don't get to decide what to do with my toys! Get your own toys to play with!

ROBERT. I don't want your stupid toys, I don't want any toys, cos I'm not a baby!

NERYS. Then why were you playing with Trevor?

ROBERT. I wasn't playing Nerys. I don't play with stupid toys!

TREVOR. Stupid, am I?

NERYS. Stupid?

ROBERT. Stupid.

TREVOR. Toy, am I?

NERYS. Fine

ROBERT. Toy!

MRS CALIGARI. *(Offstage.)* Nerys!

NERYS. What?

MRS CALIGARI. *(Offstage.)* Lesson!

NERYS. Yes!

ROBERT. Go!

NERYS. No!

TREVOR. You're a toy!

ROBERT. *(To* **TREVOR.***)* What?

NERYS. *(To* **ROBERT.***)* What?!

ROBERT. *(To* **NERYS.***)* What?!

MRS CALIGARI. *(Offstage.)* What?!

>   *(Beat.)*

NERYS AND ROBERT. Nothing!

TREVOR. And I prefer the term coin accumulation and storage receptacle.

ROBERT. Shut up!

>   *(***NERYS** *snatches up* **TREVOR.***)*

NERYS. What's wrong with you?!

TREVOR. Careful Robbie.

ROBERT. Nothing.

NERYS. Leave him alone, and just go!

TREVOR. Yes, go, please. I can't stand to look at you anymore.

NERYS. He's mine.

TREVOR. I'm hers.

NERYS. I'm going to paint him pink –

TREVOR. Huh?

NERYS. – and put a bow in his hair –

TREVOR. Now steady on –

NERYS. – and call him Jemima!

TREVOR. Kill her!

MRS CALIGARI. *(Offstage.)* Nerys, if you want to win the Annual Kent Blow-Off you need your practice poppet.

ROBERT AND NERYS. Ugh. Mum.

NERYS. I'm coming!

> *(***NERYS*** gets her recorder.)*

When I get back –

> *(She points to* ***TREVOR.****)*

– we're having crumpets.

> *(***NERYS*** skips off threateningly. There is an awkward silence.)*

ROBERT. You're not a toy.

TREVOR. You're not invited.

ROBERT. I'm sorry!

TREVOR. – and if you call *that* smart casual, well –

ROBERT. I couldn't tell her we were...we were...

TREVOR. Totally failing to murder her?

ROBERT. Argh! Trevor, I *am* a murderer, I know I am! I can be scary! It's just...every great murderer has their nemesis.

TREVOR. Every great murderer has committed murder. I'm still waiting for that...

ROBERT. *(Picking up the newspaper.)* Then wait no more. It's like you said... Look directly down the barrel of the gun, select your victim, and act.

TREVOR. Yes, YES! This is very good.

ROBERT. *(Randomly pointing at the newspaper.)* You. Mrs. Birdie Truffle, the fatty on the horse! A weapon. I need a weapon. Here – "Wanted".

> *(One by one, characters march out on stage, obscuring their faces with unfolded newspapers.)*

AGNES. Agnes Oneacre seeks oven mitts in exchange for garden shears.

ROBERT. Boring. Here!

BORIS. Boris Topple seeks plastic bag in exchange for lead pipe.

ROBERT. Predictable.

LONELY TOM. Lonely Tom seeks birthday cake in exchange for razor blades.

ROBERT. Tempting...but no.

LONELY TOM. ...I'll run the bath.

ROBERT. Hang on, there was something...

> *(Underscoring begins.)*

[SONG: "WANTED"]

IT WAS IN HERE SOMEWHERE ...

CHORUS.
WANTED

ROBERT.
WHERE IS IT?

CHORUS.
WANTED

ROBERT.
I NEED IT

CHORUS.
  WANTED

ROBERT.
  I CAN'T SEE IT

CHORUS.
  WANTED

ROBERT.
  THAT'S IT! FIFTEENTH OF JUNE

CHORUS.
  WANT IT

ROBERT.
  WEDNESDAY LAST WEEK

CHORUS.
  NEED IT.

ROBERT.
  BOTTOM OF PAGE TWO

CHORUS.
  SEE IT

ROBERT.
  BUT HOW DO I GET TO YOU?

CHORUS.
  GET IT. WANTED.

ROBERT.
  WILL EXCHANGE FOR

CHORUS.
  WANTED

EUNICE.
  WILL EXCHANGE FOR ...

CHORUS.
  WANTED

EUNICE.
ROLLERSKATES

CHORUS.
WANTED

EUNICE.
PREFERABLY GREY ...

CHORUS.
WANTED

EUNICE.
IN TIME FOR PANCAKE DAY. CONTACT EUNICE STAUNTON
BY TELEPHONE ...

CHORUS.
RING RING!

EUNICE.
WITHOUT DELAY!

CHORUS.
WANTED

EUNICE.
ROLLERSKATES

CHORUS.
WANTED

ROBERT.
ROLLER SKATES? I CAN GET THEM! WHEN WAS THE AD?
WHEN?

CHORUS.
JUNE THE FOURTH

ROBERT.
NO, NOT THEN. IT WAS A DARK AND CLOUDY DAY. IT WAS
THE FIRST, THE FIRST OF MAY!

CHORUS.
WANT IT!

ROBERT.
WHO WAS IT NOW? THINK!

CHORUS.
TIMMY?

ROBERT.
NO

CHORUS.
JERRY?

ROBERT.
NO!

CHORUS.
TERRY?

ROBERT.
NO! WAIT – YES!

TERRY.
TERRY THE FERRET MAN WILL GIVE

EUNICE.
ROLLER SKATES

TERRY.
IN EXCHANGE FOR A FERRET, A GIRLY ONE, A BREEDER

ROBERT.
THAT'S IT

CHORUS.
WANTED

ROBERT.
IT'S THERE

CHORUS.
WANTED

ROBERT.
I'M STARTING TO REMEMBER

CHORUS.
NEED IT!

REGINALD.
WOULD LIKE AN INHALER

ROBERT.
WHAT?

REGINALD.
AN INHALER, IN EXCHANGE FOR

CHORUS.
WANT IT

REGINALD.
MY HIDEOUS PET FERRET ANGELA

TERRY.
A GIRLY ONE, A BREEDER

ROBERT.
REGINALD NEEDS AN INHALER

REGINALD. *(Wheeze.)*

ROBERT.
TO EASE HIS WHEEZY CHEST, BUT WHAT'S NEXT? THINK,
JUST THINK

CHORUS.
GET IT

TERRY.
A GIRLY ONE, A BREEDER

CHORUS.
WANTED

ROBERT.
SHH, NOT NOW!

FILIDIA.
SOME BROKEN PLATES

ROBERT.
HEY WAIT!

FILIDIA.
SOME BROKEN PLATES FOR AN INHALER

REGINALD.
AN INHALER

CHORUS.
GET IT!

EUNICE.
ROLLER SKATES, PREFERABLY GREY!

CHORUS.
WANTED

ROBERT.
EUNICE, GO AWAY
BROKEN PLATES, WAIT WAIT

EUNICE.
ROLLERSKATES

TERRY.
A GIRLY ONE

GERTRUDE.
BRAND NEW PLATE IN EXCHANGE FOR

FILIDIA.
BROKEN PLATES

ROBERT.
SEE IT

CHORUS.
WANT IT

GERTRUDE.
BRAND NEW PLATE

ROBERT.
WANT IT.

CHORUS.
NEED IT

FILIDA.
BROKEN PLATES

ROBERT.
NEED IT

CHORUS.
GET IT!

ROBERT.
HA! THIS IS GREAT

TERRY.
FERRET!

ADMIRAL.
I'VE GOT A PLATE

GERTRUDE.
A BRAND NEW PLATE

EUNICE.
ROLLERSKATES

REGINALD.
INHALER

ROBERT.
SHH

TERRY.
A BREEDER

ROBERT.
QUIET, THAT MAN NEEDS A

CHORUS.
WANTED

ADMIRAL.
A CANE

CHORUS.
WANTED

ROBERT.
A CANE?

ADMIRAL.
A BLIND MAN'S CANE

FILIDIA.
PLATES

EUNICE.
SKATES

ROBERT.
WAIT, I CAN WIN THIS GAME
I JUST NEED TO FIND – A BLIND MAN'S CANE.
A BLIND MAN'S CANE. A BLIND. MAN'S. CANE. *(Gasp.)*

> *(We hear* **FRANK GRICE**, *from the first scene, leave the pub – "If you're not dead, buy the drinks!".)*

All clear, Mr Grice!

> *(The same noise from earlier of* **FRANK** *being mown down. The cane flies from the wreckage offstage landing in* **ROBERT**'s *hand. He laughs manically.)*

HAHAHAHAHAHAHA! A BLIND MAN'S CANE. IN
EXCHANGE FOR

GERTRUDE/ROBERT.
BRAND NEW PLATE

ROBERT.
IN EXCHANGE FOR

FILIDIA/ROBERT.
BROKEN PLATES

ROBERT.

IN EXCHANGE FOR

REGINALD/ROBERT.

AN INHALER

ROBERT.

IN EXCHANGE FOR

TERRY/ROBERT.

A GIRLY ONE, A BREEDER

ROBERT.

IN EXCHANGE FOR

EUNICE/ROBERT.

ROLLERSKATES

CHORUS.

IN EXCHANGE –

IN EXCHANGE –

IN EXCHANGE –

CHORUS/ROBERT.

IN EXCHANGE FOR –

EUNICE.

A CROSSBOW!

> (**EUNICE** *passes the crossbow to a gleeful* **ROBERT** *who laughs maniacally. There's a menacing rumble of thunder.*)

Scene Ten – Snipers

(**ROBERT** *is at the entrance to his lair – at the top of the burnt out tree stump. He paces back and forth with his crossbow, a colander on his head, ready for battle.* **TREVOR** *stares on at* **ROBERT**, *impassive as ever.*)

TREVOR. You seem tense, Robert.

ROBERT. What?

TREVOR. Is something the matter? I could give you a massage?

ROBERT. No. And it's Sergeant Major Robert Caligari, remember?

TREVOR. Ah yes of course, apologies.

(**ROBERT** *takes aim at a distant target, holds it for a long moment, then puts the crossbow down, frustrated.*)

ROBERT. Stop it!

TREVOR. Stop what?

ROBERT. I can feel you watching me, it's putting me off. I need total concentration while I'm sniping my victim!

TREVOR. Oh snipe away Robert please, snipe away, I won't look I promise.

(**ROBERT** *takes aims again. A moment. He lowers his crossbow again, furious. Storms over to* **TREVOR** *and turns him the other way, facing away from him. He takes aim again.*)

Is that helping?

ROBERT. Trevor!

TREVOR. Sorry!

ROBERT. *(Pretending to talk into a walkie-talkie.)* Name: Sergeant Major Robert Caligari. Location: atop the mastermind's secret lair overlooking the bridge over the motorway. Target: A large globulous mass who goes by the name of Mrs Birdie Truffle, or Fatso for short!

TREVOR. Now Robert, it could be a thyroid problem.

ROBERT. Trevor, I'm trying to concentrate! The mission is simple, execute the fatso as she goes for a daily ride on her stupid horse. A bolt through the neck should do it!

TREVOR. Delightful!

ROBERT. It is, isn't it!

TREVOR. And what then?

ROBERT. ...What?

TREVOR. Well, the aftermath of course, the throat is a... messy area. The jugular will rupture, her fluids erupting forth in a careening spiral of red.

ROBERT. Oh...

TREVOR. The horse will startle when she falls, the steed, dragging her fetid body behind it, like a big bag of cottage cheese.

ROBERT. It will?

TREVOR. And the body, what then? Will you cut it up to hide it in a derelict bathtub? Oh, it's a messy business. Buckets of gunk. I'm not sure you could handle it.

ROBERT. I could handle it!

TREVOR. And what of her children? Will you mock them when you pass them in the street? I do hope so.

ROBERT. Well...

TREVOR. You will? Look them in the eye with a stare that says "I made you an orphan, boy!"

ROBERT. ...Yes!

TREVOR. Then shoot, Robert! Spill her blood! Cut her to ribbons and dissolve her in the shed!

ROBERT. I'm going to!

TREVOR. Then do it! Prove you can!

ROBERT. *(Increasingly flustered.)* This is Sergeant Major Caligari –

TREVOR. Stop talking, child, and act!

ROBERT. He...he rests his trusty steed against his shoulder –

> *(By now, **TREVOR** is roaring, baying, he will not rest.)*

TREVOR. Enough prattle, more blood! BLOOD!

ROBERT. Be quiet! Sergeant Major –

TREVOR. Now! Kill her! Do it child!

ROBERT. I'm trying!

TREVOR. You can't do it, can you? How disappointing!

> *(**ROBERT** finally loses his temper.)*

ROBERT. SHUT UP! I'm the one doing it! I'm the murderer! Me, not you! I could shoot you too, did you think of that? Before I start my human rampage I could shoot you right between your eyes and stove your head in!

> *(**ROBERT** looks down at the long fall to the bottom of the lair, grabs **TREVOR**, and forces him to look at the void waiting beneath them.)*

Or, I could drop you! I could drop you, you stupid pig! All the way down to the bottom of the lair, so that you smash into a million pieces, and spill your coppers and your coins all over the floor and I'll never have to hear your stupid voice again! What do you think of that?

(Silence.)

What do you think of it?

*(Silence. Suddenly, for the first time, **ROBERT** is afraid. And alone.)*

Trevor?

(Silence.)

Yes. Good. Exactly. Silence. That's more like it.

*(He places **TREVOR** down, and goes back to his sniper position.)*

Awaiting confirmation and will fire at will!

*(He glances over at **TREVOR**. Nothing.)*

Preparing to fire. Trevor, aren't you going to watch...?

*(Silence. **ROBERT** has been betrayed. He is furious, upset, but there is nothing left to do except...)*

Fine!!!! This is Robert Caligari, alone on the battlefield, he needs no-one! He looks directly down the barrel, selects his victim, and...and...and...

(He fires. Gasps. Blackout. The sound of a horse being punctured, and screaming in agony.)

Scene Eleven – Pile-up

(A note on this scene – this entire scene should flow together, with no blackouts. To get in and out of each section, the scenes are interspersed with **RADIO COMMENTATORS**. *Beyond that, it's entirely up to you. Good luck, and crash well!)*

*(***RADIO 1*** enters.)*

RADIO 1. Now on Petrol FM, let's play: Whose Car is My Car?

RADIO 3. *(Offstage.)* My car?

RADIO 1. Correct!

*(***RADIO 2***, ***RADIO 3*** and ***RADIO 4*** enter, their lines beginning to overlap.)*

RADIO 2. Stay tuned to Splash FM! Bringing you all the news from ponds / and rivers across the UK.

RADIO 3. Bringing you all the news, as it happens, where it happens and even / when it doesn't happen.

RADIO 4. Up next we'll be interviewing our local butcher Clive to see how he gets those steaks so gosh darned tender –

(We snap, instantly, into a rickety bus, containing the characters from the first scene: **SALLY**, **BILLY** *and the* **OLD SEA CAPTAIN**, *driven by a* **BUS DRIVER**. *We recommend pulling their hats out of some big pockets, everyone loves a hat reveal.)*

SALLY. Turn that down will you!

BILLY. But it's Clive! They're talking about his famous blood-letting technique!

SALLY. How can you care about the radio when as we speak, our precious Frank Grice is being bundled into an incinerator!

BILLY. Oh come on Sally, you've got to think about the good times! Frank, Frank, such beautiful eyes!

SALLY. *(Almost crying.)* But not anymore –

OLD SEA CAPTAIN. COS HE'S DEAD!

(**SALLY** *weeps openly. We freeze.*)

RADIO 1. We interrupt our usual broadcast to bring you this special report from the motorways of Kent, England. It seems a horse and rider have leapt to their deaths in bizarre, species-spanning suicide pact.

RADIO 2. Next up on Boom FM, tunes to make you go "hmmm". Forgettable classics from the decades you'd rather not remember.

RADIO 3. Coming up we'll be interviewing Yorkshire's foremost crochet champion, about the dark underseam of the chunky world of knit.

RADIO 4. *(Singing a power ballad.*)*

(During the following lines, move into next scene positions.)

RADIO 1. After being hit by a crossbow bolt, the horse leapt from a bridge to the motorway below causing multiple crashes which are ongoing. More on this –

RADIO 2. More on this –

RADIO 3. More on this as we / get it.

---

* A licence to produce THE BOY WHO KICKED PIGS does not include a performance licence for any third-party or copyrighted music. Licensees should create an original composition or use music in the public domain. For further information, please see Music Use Note on page 3.

RADIO 4. More classic tunes in just a second!

> *(We now see two cars, one containing the* **DOCTOR** *and* **NURSE**, *one containing a bizarre couple of your choosing. Again, we recommend pulling out the relevant hats.)*

NURSE. Oh Doctor! I wish you'd tell me where we were going, I can hardly contain my excitement!

DOCTOR. Well try for God's sake Stephanie, I don't want urine on the leather trim.

NURSE. But it's just so romantic! Do you think we look like Richard Burton and ElizabethTaylor?

DOCTOR. I don't know, do I? I'm trying to drive!

NURSE. Oh I just feel so, so –

DOCTOR. Jesus Stephanie it's my one weekend off, do we have to talk shop?

NURSE. But we're not talking shop –

DOCTOR. Well you're talking, aren't you?! At work I allow that and you're damn lucky I do, but on our weekends away you're my woman. And I'm your man.

NURSE. Oh Charles!

DOCTOR. Doctor.

NURSE. Oh Doctor! Kiss me!

> *(***DOCTOR*** *turns to her, could this finally be their romantic moment?)*

Oh Doctor!

DOCTOR. Oh God, Stephanie!

NURSE. Oh God, Doctor!

> *(He looks disgusted.)*

DOCTOR. No, I mean OH GOD, STEPHANIE! Here, take this will you?

> *(He casually hands her his imaginary steering wheel.)*

NURSE. *(Almost to herself.)* But that's not how cars...

DOCTOR. I'm writing you a prescription. For a breath mint.

> *(He grabs back the imaginary steering wheel.)*

NURSE. I only wanted to tell you how much I lo–

DOCTOR. Try and cry quietly, would you?

> *(He reaches for the imagined radio, and turns the dial.)*

I want to listen to my stories.

> *(The scene dissolves.)*

RADIO 1. After the horse and rider jumped onto the motorway an oncoming petrol tanker / swerved into the other lane to avoid them –

RADIO 2. We're interrupting our usual programming to bring you an update on the tragedy currently causing havoc on the roads of Kent / It appears a petrol tanker has swerved into the road, causing multiple crashes which are ongoing.

RADIO 3. Police have yet to contain the area and there are warnings it will be a while until–

RADIO 4. We're trying to get someone on the scene but as yet–

ALL. More on this, as we–

> *(We are now in a minibus, full of priests.)*

FATHER MATTHEW. Question nine, fingers at the ready!

(All the priests raise their fingers, excited.)

Eyes on the road Father Luke!

FATHER LUKE. Oh! Right-o!

FATHER MATTHEW. Now then, in the words of our Father himself, thou shalt not covet thy neighbour's...what?

FATHER MARK. Ooh, ooh, spectacles!

FATHER LUKE. Crossword!

FATHER JOHN. Hands?

FATHER MARK. Thy neighbour's...

FATHER JOHN. What does covet mean?

FATHER LUKE. It's one of them tricky ones!

FATHER JOHN. It's not one of the kill ones?

MARK, LUKE, JOHN. Nah, they're the easy ones!

FATHER MATTHEW. I'm afraid I'm going to have to hurry you, Fathers. We do have a hundred and eighty seven of these Christian quiz questions to get through before I can award the winner...

the vat of communion wine!

ALL. Oooh!

FATHER LUKE. We'll be drunk on Jesus!

*(**FATHER JOHN** and **FATHER MARK** high five.)*

(The scene dissolves. This is a good point, if you need one, to get rid of any chairs you have onstage.)

RADIO 1. We're back, and a massive fireball is speeding its way / down the motorways of Kent.

RADIO 2. The death toll is rising by the second, though we are still waiting on an exact number –

RADIO 3. We have a reporter on the scene but we have yet to make contact –

> *(They screech to a halt, crashing into an invisible screen.)*

ALL. *(Singing an automotive jingle.*)*

> *(**CASSIE** enters, gesturing towards a car that contains a disgusting old couple: **MR** and **MRS PARP**, and what appears to be (from his gestures) the family dog, **PARP JR**. Throughout the following, **PARP JR** pants, **MRS PARP** has a terrifying smile, **MR PARP** seems to long only for furious death.)*

CASSIE. Thanks Dave. I'm here on the banks of the M2 where hundreds are attempting to flee from the fireball currently threatening to engulf Kent. One such couple have locked themselves in their Morris Minor despite the fact that it is struggling to get up a very steep bank away from the flames. Mr. Parp, can you please tell us why you're set on staying where you are?

MR PARP. I'm not leaving her! She's been with me for thirty years, I'd be nothing without her!

CASSIE. Oh, how romantic! But Mr Parp, your wife can join you as you flee the scene!

MR PARP. What? I'm talking about the car you idiot! *(He nods towards his wife.)* I hope THAT miserable harpy burns to death! Third gear!

> *(**MRS PARP** switches the gearstick to third gear.)*

---

* A licence to produce THE BOY WHO KICKED PIGS does not include a performance licence for any third-party or copyrighted music. Licensees should create an original composition or use music in the public domain. For further information, please see Music Use Note on page 3.

CASSIE. Oh Mr Parp, that's the grief talking – pre-emptive grief for the demise of your lovely wife. Hmm?

MR PARP. *(Roaring.)* Her horrible face melting into flames is the only bright spot on the horizon to be honest with you! Every day I wake up to her face next to me and think I got drunk the night before and went to bed with Satan!

CASSIE. Mr Parp, at least save your dog!

> *(All three **PARP** family members gasp in disbelief.)*

MR PARP. ...That's my son!

> *(**PARP JR** howls.)*

CASSIE. Back to you, Dave.

> *(**PARP JR** howls again.)*

DAVE?

> *(The scene dissolves.)*

RADIO 1. The flaming tanker has hit a chicken cart sending / chargrilled nuggets into the screaming crowds.

RADIO 2. Blood and feathers is all we can see from our post on the banks / of the M2.

CASSIE. I'm struggling to hear you over the din, Dave.

RADIO 3. With all the burning chicken and wine it's smelling a lot like coq au vin down here!

> *(**RADIO 3** laughs into the sudden silence. An awkward moment – a delay – then all laugh with him as if only just hearing the joke due to lag, before gasping at the sight ahead.)*

RADIO 1. It's gonna blow!

CASSIE. Oh my God!

RADIO 3. I can't breathe for the smoke!

RADIO 2. Any second now we'll all be–

RADIO 1. Please!

RADIO 2. Somebody!

CASSIE. Dave!

RADIO 3. Help!

ALL. *(Singing a pop tune.*)*

> (**DOCTOR** *and* **NURSE** *are back in their car, all of the worlds are starting to merge now, as mixed and deranged as possible.)*

NURSE. Oh Doctor! Take me in your arms for our final moments!

DOCTOR. For God's sake Stephanie stop making such a fuss!

RADIO 1. There's too much smoke!

DOCTOR. It's just like you to overreact! Alright flames, bring it on! I'm a doctor!

NURSE. *(Screaming.)* No!

RADIO 1. A couple in a red Lamborghini have just accelerated into the fireball!

RADIO 4. That is definitely game over!

> *(We are back on the minibus with the* **BUS DRIVER, SALLY, BILLY** *and the* **OLD SEA CAPTAIN***.)*

SALLY. We'll see you soon Frank!

---

* A licence to produce THE BOY WHO KICKED PIGS does not include a performance licence for any third-party or copyrighted music. Licensees should create an original composition or use music in the public domain. For further information, please see Music Use Note on page 3.

BILLY. Hang on Sally!

OLD SEA CAPTAIN. Bury me at sea!

(They all scream.)

RADIO 3. And that is R.I.P. for those O.A.P.'s

RADIO 4. Inappropriate Bill!

RADIO 3. No, in a minibus, Mark.

*(We swing back into the **PARPS**' car, almost engulfed by flames.)*

MR PARP. We need to lose some weight! Out you go, she-devil!

*(He goes to push **MRS PARP** out of the car, she screams like a demon, sprouts many arms and pulls him with her down into oblivion.)*

(The following is a heaving sea of limbs and noise, as all hell threatens to break loose.)

RADIO 4. You join me back at the studio / we have lost contact with all our reporters at the scene –

RADIO 1. We're doing as best we can, but the blood makes it difficult / to see exactly what's happening –

RADIO 3. If anyone has any idea how to get out of this hellscape, please/ please tell my wife I love–

RADIO 2. *(Weeps gently throughout the above.)*

(As the panicked hubbub grows to a fever pitch, the mass suddenly transforms into the cheerful bus of vicars, all fingers in the air, ready to answer the quiz questions.)

FATHER MATTHEW. OK Fathers, fingers at the ready! Question one hundred and eighty seven, this is for the wine. Who died for all our sins?

(All go to answer, then pause. Stumped.)

FATHER MARK. Now then –

FATHER LUKE. Goodness gracious!

FATHER MATTHEW. Quite an easy one.

FATHER JOHN. Who DID die for our sins?

FATHER MARK. Oh oh, I know, that chap, lovely dress, he–

FATHER LUKE. Tip of the tongue.

FATHER MATTHEW. One of the main characters...

> *(All at once, they see the carnage ahead. They point. Just before they are engulfed in the twisted blaze.)*

ALL. JESUS CHRIST!

> *(Explosion.)*

> *(Blackout.)*

Scene Twelve – The Fall

(Back at the entrance to **ROBERT***'s lair, just as it was before the carnage.* **ROBERT** *stands, with his crossbow, looking amazed. After a beat, he explodes with delight.)*

ROBERT. I did it! I did it! I did it!! Did you see Trevor? Did you see the way they burnt, screaming and dancing in the flames? All because of me! Me, Trevor, me!

(He picks up **TREVOR***, and perches on the edge of the lair.)*

So, whose tune am I dancing to now, hey Trevor? Whose tune? WHOSE TUNE?

(In his passion, **ROBERT** *nearly tumbles into the dark hole below. He steadies himself. Then grins. He's had an idea.)*

What was it you said Trevor? A real murderer looks his victim right between the eyes and makes a pact with the soul he is about to claim?

(He stares **TREVOR** *in the eyes, and dangles him over the edge of the lair.)*

Well. Goodbye Trevor!

(He goes to drop him in, and a sudden lightning flash startles him. **ROBERT** *screams, and tumbles down, down, down, to the bottom of the lair, his screams echoing as he falls. We do not hear him land.)*

Scene Thirteen – The Kent Clarion

*(Back in the Kent Clarion office, the clock ticking, **WENDY**, **THOMAS** and **PHILIP** all in their original positions. **THOMAS** sighs, heavily. **WENDY** checks the phone. **PHILIP** struggles to contain his pent up frustration. It's clear they have had nothing to do for some time.)*

THOMAS. Nothing...incoming, Wendy?

WENDY. Not a peep Thomas, not a sausage of a peep!

THOMAS. These are dark days Wendy, and no mistake!

*(**PHILIP** can't take it anymore. He is finally ready to let it all out.)*

PHILIP. OH SHUT UP, WILL YOU SHUT UP, BOTH OF YOU! How can you live like this? This endless nothingness, I can't take it!!

WENDY. Now Philip, I think you ought to –

PHILIP. Anything! I will write anything! Something has to have happened, something has to have–

THOMAS. Philip, I'm afraid we can't simply conjure up a parade just because you've asked for one!

PHILIP. I'm not asking for a parade, I just want something to look at, to, to think about, to comment on! Something juicy, something delicious, something...

(He suddenly realises what he wants.)

...terrible.

WENDY. Terrible, Philip? But I thought you said –

PHILIP. I know what I said! I take it all back, you were right about bad news, we need it! We feed on it! Just one disaster, that's all I ask, just one tiny, delicious, juicy disaster and I'll –

> *(The telephone rings.* **WENDY** *goes to answer it,* **PHILIP** *wrenches the phone from her hand, furious and triumphant.)*

(Shouting.) Hello Kent Clarion, Philip Bottering speaking, anything dreadful happen?

> *(A pause as he listens.)*

WENDY. Well done young man!

THOMAS. He's getting the hang of this, isn't he?

> *(***PHILIP*** *shushes her. He listens to the other end of the phone, excited.)*

PHILIP. Yes? Terrible accident! Wait, flaming chickens? And wine?!

> *(He continues to listen. The news begins to sink in. The triumph begins to falter, and fade.)*

Sorry, what do you –

> *(Beat.)*

...hundreds dead? Oh my God. Yes. Yes, of course. We'll be right there.

> *(He puts the phone down, gently. A heavy silence.)*

WENDY. *(Jovially.)* So that was flaming chickens in exchange for –

PHILIP. No! No. There's...there's been an accident, on the motorway. A huge fire, she said, coming this way.

WENDY. A fire?

THOMAS. Oh do come on, young man.

PHILIP. It's just down the road. Are you coming?

WENDY. I'm sorry?

PHILIP. Well, shouldn't we get down there? Live reporting?

THOMAS. Leave the office, you mean?

WENDY. But what if someone calls, we can't leave the phone off the hook?

PHILIP. But THIS IS NEWS!

(A beat. THOMAS and WENDY burst into peals of laughter.)

WENDY. News! Around here?!

THOMAS. Very good, young man!

PHILIP. This is a disaster on our doorstep! We'll be the first at the scene!

(WENDY and THOMAS are suddenly deadly serious.)

WENDY. I see. Looking for a scoop in our first week, are we?

THOMAS. *(Menacingly.)* Twenty years I waited –

WENDY. Twenty years he waited –

THOMAS. For my first scoop.

WENDY. His first one.

THOMAS. A page four scoop.

WENDY. Headline news.

(THOMAS is now leaning threateningly over PHILIP.)

THOMAS. So there's no rush, young Peter.

PHILIP. *(Terrified.)* It's... Philip!

THOMAS. No rush at all.

WENDY. No need to fabricate an apocalyptic scene –

PHILIP. But it's not fabricated!

> (**THOMAS** *loses his temper completely.*)

THOMAS. THAT'S ENOUGH, YOUNG MAN!

> (*All three sit back down.* **THOMAS** *fuming,*
> **PHILIP** *upset and defeated,* **WENDY** *mildly*
> *aroused by* **THOMAS***'s outburst. They sit.*
> *Waiting. Gradually, the crackling sounds of*
> *fire begin to filter in. They begin to sniff the*
> *air, intrigued.*)

What...what is that?

WENDY. Smells awfully scrummy.

THOMAS. Not your lunch?

WENDY. No, I brought spam.

> (**PHILIP** *gasps, suddenly seeing the roaring*
> *fireball making its way towards them. He is*
> *too afraid to speak, but points and moans.*)

THOMAS. It smells like...gosh, it smells awfully like –

> (*They all gasp, as the flames burst through*
> *the doors.*)

ALL. COQ AU VIN!

Scene Fourteen – The Bottom of the Lair

(During the following voice over, the lights very gradually come up on the bottom of **ROBERT***'s horrible lair to reveal him impaled by many spikes.* **TREVOR** *is on the ground nearby, tipped over.* **ROBERT** *is obviously in immense pain.)*

DAVE. *(Offstage.)* In other news disruptive scenes at the Annual Kent Blow-Off. Nerys Caligari, rising star of the recorder world, was performing a particularly vigorous passage of Bach's Recorder Concerto in F, when her head exploded. Police have found unnatural levels of weedkiller in her blood, which they are treating as unsuspicious. Blow-Off Judge Nigel Toot said, "It was all going rather well, until she decided to show off." Coming up next – !

(We can now see **ROBERT** *clearly. He moans, gasps, in pain and panic. He spots* **TREVOR** *next to him.)*

ROBERT. Trevor! ...Trevor! ...Help me! What shall I do Trevor? What shall I do?

*(***CALLUM***, a well-dressed gentleman enters. He is immaculate, well-spoken, immensely calm, but there's something off about him...)*

CALLUM. Hello!

ROBERT. Who are you?!

CALLUM. Oh, just a passerby.

ROBERT. Please help me! Please, these branches, I think they've gone straight through me!

CALLUM. Gosh, yes, they have rather. That must be awfully painful for you.

ROBERT. Yes!

CALLUM. What can I do for you, do you need directions, or –

ROBERT. What? No, please, just listen –

CALLUM. Of course, where are my manners, you were saying?

ROBERT. Please, please just lift me off! There's so much blood...and it...hurts!

CALLUM. What, me?!

ROBERT. Yes!

CALLUM. My dear chap, I'm afraid there's been some sort of mistake –

ROBERT. I'm begging you –

CALLUM. Dear fellow – hate to be the bearer for bad news and all, but I must implore you to look a little more closely...

(*Beat. He gestures to himself.*)

I'm a rat.

(*Beat.*)

(*Spoken, definitely not squeaked.*) Squeak.

ROBERT. ...What?

CALLUM. I'm a rat, dear boy, you've heard of us, yes?

ROBERT. A...a rat?

CALLUM. Sewer creepers, litter eaters, corner festerers, floorboard pesterers, plague bringers, squeal singers, shoe encumberers, Hamlin's numberers – you've heard of us, yes?

ROBERT. But rats don't t–

(He cries out in pain. **CALLUM** *remains unruffled.)*

CALLUM. Dear, oh dear, that does sound nasty. Yes, so... sorry old thing. Not really my strong suit, the old Achillean might. Don't have the relevant elbow joints you see and to be honest I'm dreadful over the phone!

(A pause while he stares at the boy. He is thoughtful suddenly.)

But do let me know if you need someone to...clean up after it's all...over. Let you bleed out a little and you will be delicious.

*(***CALLUM*** *runs a finger down* **ROBERT**'*s face, to catch a drop of blood. As he begins to walk away, he gently tastes the blood and stops.)*

On second thought –

(A moment of radio static is heard, and during the following **CALLUM** *begins to advance on* **ROBERT**, *who starts to plead and cry for his life.)*

DAVE. *(Offstage.) (Cheerful.)* Well, this is truly a dark day for Kent and even beyond. Police at the scene are estimating the death toll at nearly two hundred already and the inferno continues to blaze!

ROBERT. *(Panicked.)* No! Please! Wait, you can't! I turned against the human race, I'm one of you, Mr... Mr...

*(***CALLUM*** *goes to shake his hand.)*

CALLUM. Callum!

*(***ROBERT*** *shrieks in pain at the touch.)*

(Radio static again. The lights mirror the hazy confusion. As we hear the below **CALLUM**

circles the boy, taking in the sights, the smells, joyfully, as **ROBERT** *continues to suffer.)*

DAVE. *(Offstage.)* I think it's only right that we take a minute now to think about what's happened today. A moment to pause and reflect on the lives lost and the chaos caused. So, this is for them –

(The opening notes of a track drift in. It is a song in the style of **"PERFECT DAY"** *by Lou Reed.* It plays until the very end of the show. It should steer them towards using something romantic, which you can waltz to.)*

– for them, and their families, to let them know that we're thinking about them at this difficult time.

CALLUM. I do appreciate your noble gesture child, I really do. It is so refreshing to have one of your kind so eager to jump aboard our ship, but you must know it counts for nothing. You're too flighty and we're too... hungry!

*(***ROBERT** *is by now openly weeping.* **CALLUM** *breathes in the smoke, hungrily, and listens to the music.)*

Your smell boy! The flesh and the smoke!

ROBERT. Please! Please don't do this!

CALLUM. Music does the most incredible things to the appetite! Don't you think?

(As the first chorus of a song in the style of **"PERFECT DAY"** *by Lou Reed* hits,* **CALLUM** *hisses, all his charm gone, and dives like an animal onto* **ROBERT**, *beginning to devour him. A spray of blood careens into the air.* **ROBERT** *screams.* **CALLUM**'s *face is covered in blood.)*

(As the chorus ends, **FELICITY**, *a well-dressed woman, the perfect partner to* **CALLUM**, *enters.)*

FELICITY. Callum? I thought I heard a scream –

(She surveys the scene, as **ROBERT** *gently moans.)*

What's all this?

CALLUM. Why it's a gift, darling! For you. And for me

FELICITY. Why?

CALLUM. Oh, did you think I'd forgotten?

(He grabs her and spins her.)

Happy anniversary darling!

(They embrace.)

FELICITY. Oh Callum! It's perfect! How did you know?

(They begin to waltz to the music.)

---

* A licence to produce THE BOY WHO KICKED PIGS does not include a performance licence for "PERFECT DAY". The publisher and author suggest that the licensee contact PRS to ascertain the music publisher and contact such music publisher to license or acquire permission for performance of the song. If a licence or permission is unattainable for "PERFECT DAY", the licensee may not use the song in THE BOY WHO KICKED PIGS but should create an original composition in a similar style or use a similar song in the public domain. For further information, please see Music Use Note on page 3.

CALLUM. Call it...an animal instinct. And you know how
I've always loved you in red.

FELICITY. Oh Callum! I love you, Callum

CALLUM. And I you, Felicity!

> (*A song in the style of* **"PERFECT DAY"**
> *by Lou Reed* is about to reach the chorus
> once again. The rats approach* **ROBERT**,
> *triumphant, greedy, mad, as he begs them,
> incoherently, to stop.*)

Shall we darling? SHALL WE?

ROBERT. No, NO!

> (*The chorus hits. The rats feast noisily. The
> blood spurts, gushes, ideally hitting the
> audience in splatters. The boy screams. The
> innards come out. It is beautifully horrific.*)

> (*A flash of lightning, a roll of thunder, and the
> rats – covered in blood – hiss into the sudden
> light, scurrying away into the darkness.*)

> (*Our horrible hero gasps his final, choking
> breaths, and then is still, as the song finally
> begins to fade.*)

> (*As the lights fade down, we are jolted into
> light by a final rush of static.*)

---

* A licence to produce THE BOY WHO KICKED PIGS does not include
a performance licence for "PERFECT DAY". The publisher and author
suggest that the licensee contact PRS to ascertain the music publisher
and contact such music publisher to license or acquire permission for
performance of the song. If a licence or permission is unattainable for
"PERFECT DAY", the licensee may not use the song in THE BOY WHO
KICKED PIGS but should create an original composition in a similar
style or use a similar song in the public domain. For further information,
please see Music Use Note on page 3.

DAVE. *(Offstage.) (Triumphantly.)* More on this horrifying
     story...as we get it!

    (Blackout.)

The End

PROPS LIST

Scene One – Frank
Blind man's cane
Tankard
Vase with flowers
Braided pigtail

Scene Two – Kent Clarion
Telephone

Scene Three – The Caligaris'
Newspaper
Recorder
Trevor, an oversized piggy bank

Scene Six – Doctor's
Clipboard
Stethoscope
Lollipop

Scene Seven – The Lair
Newspaper
Recorder
Trevor

Scene Eight – Pedro
Newspaper
Radio
Beach towel
Beach buckets and spades
Framed picture of Pedro

Scene Nine – Weedkiller
Trevor
A bonnet for Trevor (removable)
Children's tea set
Recorder
Newspapers × 4

Blind man's cane
Crossbow

Scene Ten – Snipers
Crossbow
Colander
Trevor

Scene Twelve – The Fall
Crossbow
Colander
Trevor

Scene Thirteen– The Kent Clarion
Telephone

Scene Fourteen – The Bottom of the Lair
Trevor
As much blood and guts (we recommend some lovely
    intestines) as you like

LIGHTING

Scene One – Frank
A small central spot, cold
Flash of face light – car crash
Snap blackout

Scene Two – Kent Clarion
Stage wash, cold
Face light, cold
Cut to –

Scene Three – The Caligaris'
Stage wash, cold
Face light, cold
Snap blackout – pig kick

Scene Four – Coppers
Lights up
Stage wash, cold
Face light, cold
Fade to black as Coppers exit

Scene Five – Community Service
4 × hard-edged spots, shaped like rectangular doorways,
    front on to cast
Generic face light, cold – opens as cast use stage
Fade to black as cast exit

Scene Six – Doctor's
Stage wash, cold
Face light, cold
Snap blackout – final line

Scene Seven – The Lair
Gobo – broken tree branches from above, cold. Low at
    first, grows throughout scene
Low face light, cold
Snap blackout – final line

Scene Eight – Pedro
Small spot, Philip alone
Stage wash, cold – as scene shifts to beach
Face light, cold
Fade back to spot as Philip returns to office
Fade to black

Scene Nine – Weedkiller
Stage wash, cold
Face light, cold
Flashes of lightning, throughout song
Large flash and blackout – "A crossbow!"

Scene Ten – Snipers
Stage wash, cold
Face light, cold
Snap to black – final line

Scene Eleven – Pile-up
Stage wash, cold
Face light, cold
Small spots highlight certain cars, flashing on and off as
    focus shifts between them
Bright flash of face light – "Jesus Christ!" P73
Snap to black

Scene Twelve – The Fall
Stage wash, cold
Face light, cold
Fade as Robert falls into the lair

Scene Thirteen – Kent Clarion
Stage wash, cold
Face light, cold
Bright flash of face light – "Coq au vin!" P78
Snap to black

Scene Fourteen – The Bottom of the Lair
Gobo – broken tree branches from above, cold. Low at
  first, grows throughout scene
Low face light, cold
Small red spot grows as the rats devour Robert
Flashes of cold lightning
Fade slowly to black

SOUND

Scene One – Frank
A high-pitched female scream
Screech of tires, vehicle braking, car horn, a smash and
thump

Scene Two – Kent Clarion
Typewriter tapping
Telephone ring

Scene Four – Coppers
Radio tuning in
A blender

Scene Six – Doctor's
Heart monitor

Scene Eight – Pedro
Radio tuning in

Scene Nine – Weedkiller
Repeat of car effect from Scene 1
Rumble of thunder

Scene Ten – Snipers
Crossbow firing
Horse being hit with arrow and whinnying

Scene Eleven – Pile-up
Radio static and tuning used throughout for transitions
Explosion

Scene Twelve – The Fall
Crack of lightning

Scene Thirteen – Kent Clarion
Clock ticking
Telephone ring

Crackling sounds of fire
Explosion of flames

Scene Fourteen – The Bottom of the Lair
Radio static
Thunder and lightning

ABOUT THE AUTHOR

Kill the Beast are Dave, Tash, Ollie, Zoe and Clem. Having met at University of Warwick, they are a collection of five writers and actors who have written for stage, TV and radio, winning awards, acclaim and a string of high profile lovers in the process.

Since their formation in 2011, they have written and produced four hugely successful, critically-acclaimed theatre shows (*The Boy Who Kicked Pigs*, *He Had Hairy Hands*, *Don't Wake The Damp* and *Director's Cut*) and several chart-topping podcasts.

Community Service

Words and Music by
KILL THE BEAST

Bouncy, furtive and just a little slinky ♩ = 125

Suggested bass line.
Repeats throughout entire song.

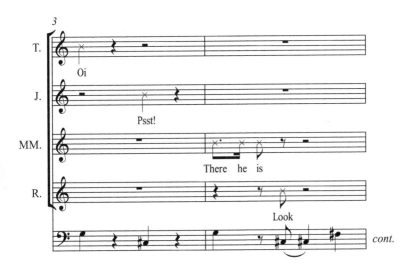

cont.

A

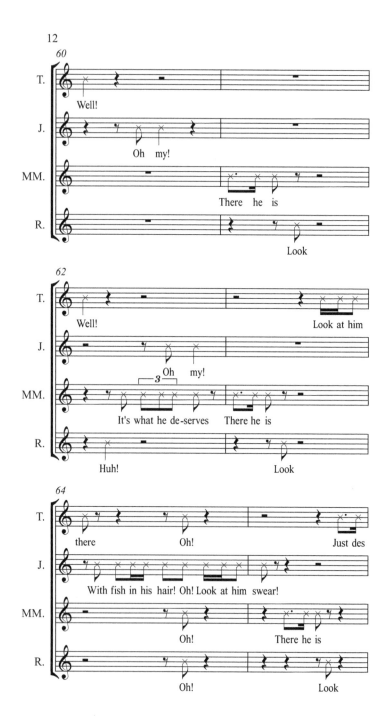

5

Wanted

Words and Music by
KILL THE BEAST

Dark, bubbling excitment ♩ = 125

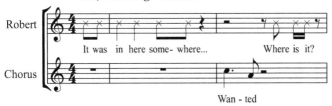

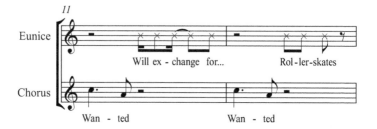

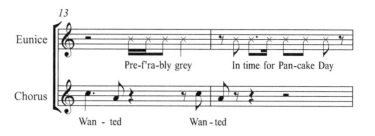

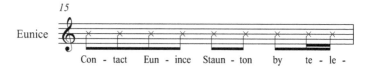

Robert: Rol-ler skates? I can get them! When was the ad? When?

Chorus: Wan - ted

Robert: No— not then it was a dark and clou-dy day

Chorus: June the fourth

Robert: It was the first, the first of May! Who was it now? Think!

Chorus: Want it

Robert: No. No. No, wait, yes!

Chorus: Tim- my? Jer- ry? Ter- ry?

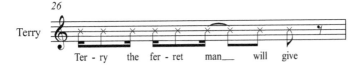

Terry: Ter - ry the fer - ret man— will give

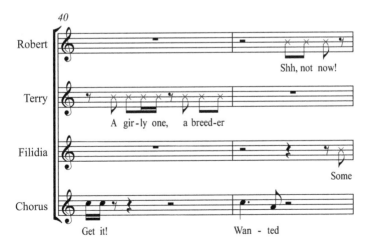

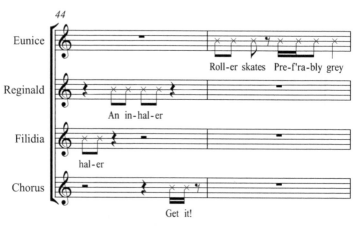

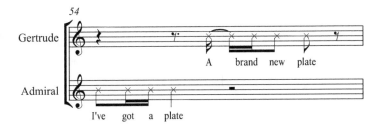

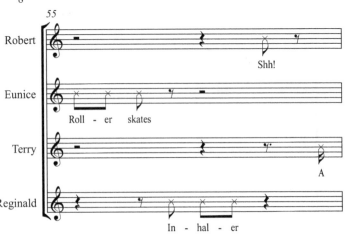

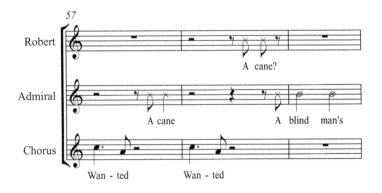

9

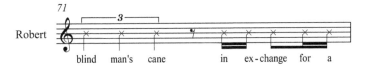

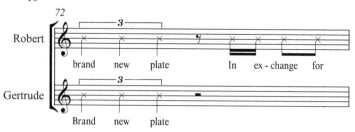

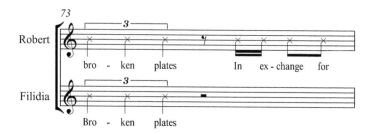

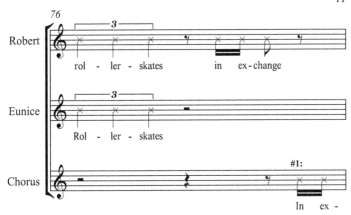

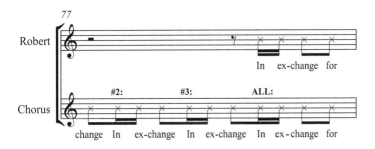

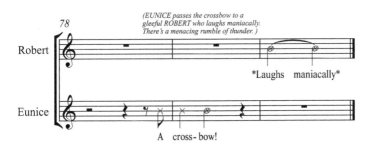

CPSIA information can be obtained
at www.ICGtesting.com
Printed in the USA
BVHW041423071220
595089BV00002B/277